Always on Sunday

Always on Sunday

Ed Sullivan: An Inside View

by MICHAEL DAVID HARRIS

MEREDITH PRESS / **New York**

First edition

Library of Congress Catalog Card Number: 68-19031

MANUFACTURED IN THE UNITED STATES OF AMERICA FOR MEREDITH PRESS

VAN REES PRESS • NEW YORK

To WEH, WEH, Jr., and LB

For unshakable friendship
Always on Sunday through Saturday

Contents

Always on Sunday

1

Let's Hear It for What's His Name

If critics could kill, Ed Sullivan would be a corpse. In 1948 television writers laughed at his appearance and personality, predicting he would never be a polished host and he couldn't last out the year. They were partially correct. The unsmiling Irishman has had the last laugh, but his lack of smoothness still inspires caricature. Today the awkward introduction is a trademark, and people react with warmth and not irritation to the most unintentionally hilarious ad libs on television.

"Ed Sullivan has introduced me as Jack Carson, John Crater, John Kerr and Carson McCullers," Jack Carter said. "Now I have my contracts with him made out 'to whom it may concern.'"

There was the time he said: "Let's hear it for the Lord's Prayer" after Sergio Franchi sang it on the 1965 Christmas show. He introduced Roberta Sherwood as Roberta Peters, New Zealand natives became "the fierce Maori tribe from New England," and a word on behalf of the tuberculosis drive ended up as "Good night and help stamp out TV." When his producer and son-in-law Bob Precht went home

3

sick one Sunday afternoon, Sullivan extended on the air get-well wishes to his "producer Bob Hope." He presented "Eileen O'Farrell of the Met" and "the Samoans from Samoa" and said "I'd like to prevent Robert Merrill." A very much alive composer became the late Irving Berlin; Walter Winchell was a "sports star," and clarinetist Benny Goodman, a "trumpeter." He has introduced Robert Goulet so many times as a Canadian that few people besides Goulet himself are aware that the singer was born in Massachusetts. He presented the Supremes with a lengthy and flattering description of their abilities, but after he finished the introduction and brought them on camera he forgot the group's name. "Here are the girls," he said.

When Michigan State won the Big-Ten championship and Sullivan had the team on his stage, he kept referring to the school as the University of Michigan. They did not correct him. The football players went home and sent Sullivan a huge birthday cake, and on it his name was misspelled.

Sullivan called over Jack Jones at dress rehearsal and asked, "Wasn't Allan Jones your father?" "He still is," the singer replied. The line got a big laugh from the studio audience and the host told Jones he wanted to keep it in the show. At night he asked, "Is your father still alive?"

Sullivan and Richard Hearne spent a Saturday afternoon rehearsing an introduction to the comedian's famous "passing out ceremony." In the script, Hearne explains that he's performed it nineteen times on the show and would like to try something new, the conjurer's routine. This is Sullivan's cue to persuade the comic into doing the old sketch one more time because it's still funny. On air, when

Hearne proposed the conjurer's routine, Sullivan replied, "Fine, Dick. Go ahead. Let's see it."

Sometimes he makes mistakes when he tries to correct his mistakes. He presented the All-America football team of 1966 and identified the wrong man as quarterback Steve Spurrier of the University of Florida. When the CBS switchboard jammed up with protest calls from Florida, Sullivan decided to correct his error. "Oh, I understand we got a call from Florida that we didn't get the picture of that big Spurrier. Is he here? Bring him on. University of Miami didn't get on." Then he brought the right Spurrier on stage but the switchboard lit up all over again as University of Florida people complained over the plug for the wrong school, their University of Miami rival. Later in the same show he corrected his correction casually as he introduced singer Glen Yarborough's number. "Steve Spurrier, the big guy, you know, from the University of Florida says they are all waiting for you to sing . . ."

When Hollywood did a remake of *Stagecoach,* the producers booked a fast-draw artist from the film, Thell Reed, Jr., in order to get a plug. Sullivan presented Reed but forgot to mention the name of the motion picture. After the show he learned of his omission and said he would correct the mistake on the following Sunday by talking about Reed again. He remembered to bring up Reed but forgot to mention the name of the film a second time.

The most awkward sponsor goof came when he was advertising Kent cigarettes on the show. Congress was pressuring the tobacco firms not to gear their advertising to youngsters, and Kent asked to have their commercials kept away from acts that appealed to teen-agers, such as rock-and-roll groups. During one week the Senate

Commerce Committee made life for the industry particularly tense. On that Sunday an agency man took special care over the placing of the commercial. Veteran musical-comedy performer Blossom Seeley was on the show, and when Sullivan put the commercial before her number, the agency was especially pleased. "We're safe," said the man from Lennen and Newell. "Senator Magnuson can't complain about this one." On air Sullivan ad-libbed his introduction of Miss Seeley: "Before all of you young people can see a veteran in action, here's a word from Kent cigarettes."

There was the Sunday when dancers were finishing the show with the Stop Op Dance, a number Sullivan brought back from Monte Carlo. The program was running short and Sullivan needed to fill up the extra time. Without checking his producer first, he walked over to the onstage musicians and asked them to play the song once more. He was unaware that the music had been pre-recorded and the band was faking it. The musicians were forced to play live and fortunately were successful enough so that the audience did not realize anything was wrong.

He came downstairs from his dressing room on the night of a live show in June, 1967. It was a quarter of, and he wanted to know why Robert Goulet, who was opening the program, was not backstage and ready to go on. A staff member explained to Sullivan that he had misread his watch and it was quarter to seven, not quarter to eight.

It is ironic that a man who is unaware of the correct hour has known exactly what time it is for two decades. His mistakes on camera may make him appear foolish, but underneath the facade lies a shrewd and serious showman. His is the most unusual success story in the history of a very unusual medium, the spectacle of the loser who wins every week. From his suite in Delmonico's Hotel at 59th Street and Park Avenue in New York, he presides over one of America's best-known institutions, and he has parlayed an uncanny awareness of the public taste into a multimillion dollar enterprise. He has defied all predictions by reaching the top and staying there, through intelligence and determination. As *Time* magazine put it, "Ed Sullivan is the longest shot to have paid off in show business."

Ed and Sylvia Sullivan have called the Delmonico home for more than twenty years. The office and apartment are combined in one suite of rooms on the eleventh floor. There are two doors at the end of the hall to the left of the elevator. The left door is the office, Room 1101. The apartment, 1102, is on the right.

In the office are three desks, hundreds of books, a rolled-up movie screen, scattered papers, a large silver shoe— a "really big shew" given to Sullivan by the Academy of Television Arts and Sciences—and a few trophies and awards of the hundreds he's won. On the wall is an autographed picture of Cardinal Spellman, *Time* magazine's cover of Sullivan, photographs of the family and of celebrities as they appeared on the show—Maurice Chevalier, Ella Fitzgerald, Bill Robinson, Robert E. Sherwood, Raymond Massey, Cole Porter, Monty Woolley, Humphrey Bogart, Lauren Bacall, Richard Burton, Robert Goulet, Julie Andrews—and a drawing by Walt Disney of Sullivan playing golf with Donald Duck, a gift from the artist. Sullivan is also playing golf in a photograph inside a heavy silver frame which was a present from Jerry Lewis. When it originally arrived, it contained Jerry Lewis' picture.

The door to 1102 opens onto a foyer and then a living

room where Sullivan is host to his guests. This adjoins a sitting room and a hallway which leads to two bedrooms and connects with 1101. The suite was once three separate apartments, but walls were knocked down until today the Sullivans occupy six rooms.

The most striking thing about the apartment, besides numerous books, is the many paintings on the wall. There are about forty, and when they travel Mrs. Sullivan visits the galleries and often ships new ones home. The most valuable are a Renoir (a twenty-fifth anniversary present from Ed which Sylvia selected), a Vlaminck, a Bombois and a small Gauguin. Others are by Xavier Cugat—the strolling violinist and caricaturist on the night the Sullivans met—and Aldo Affortunati, whose painting—a European country road—is Ed's favorite. Once Harry Belafonte admired a picture and Sullivan took it off the wall and gave it to him.

The apartment is tastefully furnished and does not have a decorator look. In the living room there is a blue-and-green tufted sofa in a silk fabric with matching throw pillows and French chairs upholstered in green satin on either side. In front is an Italian coffee table with a brown painted top resembling marble and a gold Greek key design around the edge. The bookcases are modern and mirrored, and there is an artificial plant and a real split philodendron on a high brass trivet. Off-white antique satin draperies decorate the windows of both the living room and the adjoining sitting room, where Mrs. Sullivan has her canasta games. There the sofa is upholstered in red and the bridge table has a green leather top with tulling and chairs to match. The Sullivans' bedroom has a French feel. The colors are muted—off-white with touches of blue and green. The den, which used to be their daughter Betty's room, has Chinese chests with a red lacquer finish. In its total effect, the apartment is more homey than elegant.

There is only one recognizable memento of Sullivan's television career outside of the office, a velvet-lined box on a bookcase in the living room. It contains a small metal replica of the placque put up in his studio when the name was changed to The Ed Sullivan Theater. The inscription reads: "This theater is dedicated to and named for Ed Sullivan, one of America's great showmen, in honor of his unique contribution to the nation's entertainment over the past twenty years. The CBS Television Network. December 10, 1967."

Sullivan conducts most of his business during the day over the telephone, speaking to agents, performers and "The Ed Sullivan Show" office in the CBS Broadcast Center. He tries not to make appointments more than a few days in advance, and all except the most important are subject to reconfirmation. He is liable to cancel everything on his schedule at the last minute. Sullivan seldom sees the guests on his show before Sunday unless he drops in to look at their nightclub acts. He never goes to rehearsals during the week and the stars don't expect it (except for Debbie Reynolds, who was "hurt").

There have been many interesting stories written about the excitement that goes on in Suite 1102. They describe the time that Sullivan had Ezio Pinza surprise Sylvia outside the door by singing "Some Enchanted Evening" and the afternoon Elvis Presley walked in the room while Mrs. Sullivan was playing cards with her friends. The anecdotes make good copy but are not typical of the atmosphere. It is so quiet and there are so few visitors that at least three of his secretaries have quit out of boredom (and he has only had half a dozen).

"Sylvia and I live a surprisingly quiet life. We live, in fact, just about the way we lived on my newspaper salary. We go to the theater a lot and dine alone about five nights a week. Sylvia, like any other doting grandmother, visits the grandchildren not less than twice a week, and she continues to work for the Service League of the United Public Health Service Hospitals of which she is president. My big diversion is golf." This was in 1960 and things have not changed much since then.

Sullivan likes freedom and spontaneity and hates to feel closed in. He was infuriated once by a reporter who told him, "I want to sit in your pocket. . . . I want to follow you everywhere." The reporter never did the story.

Sylvia says, "Ed and I now live the kind of flexible life we both want to lead. Ed's always had to adhere to deadlines as a newspaper man and on TV, but in our private lives we like the freedom to do what we please at any hour we please. We don't socialize because we're not the dinner-party type. It's poison for Ed to know that he has to go to somebody's house for dinner. We're not interested in making the social scene, the 'must' parties. We never go to cocktail parties and seldom to formal dinners. When we do, it is usually on the spur of the moment. Ed hates to have a tied-down feeling. I think if he wants to take a nap at seven o'clock and eat at ten o'clock, he should be able to do it. Nothing infuriates him more than to *have* to be at a certain place at a certain time. He has enough of this in his work."

Hotel living has suited their needs perfectly and dates back to the days when Sullivan was putting on vaudeville

shows at Loew's State. They moved into the Hotel Astor
because the deadlines and late hours made it convenient
to be around the corner. Sylvia says, "It was nice not
to worry about housekeeping because we treasured our
leisure time. We developed quite a taste for dining out. We
still do every night of the week. . . . I have never known any
other way of life."

They never entertain at home but in restaurants. "We
like gay places," she says, and they go to Le Club, the
Colony, Le Pavillon, Luchow's, Dinty Moore's, Capri, Le-
one's, Romeo Salta, La Grenouille and Danny's Hideaway.
Sylvia is a gourmet. Ed had a series of collisions and broken
noses playing football in high school, and it left him with
hardly any sense of smell. As a result he cannot taste most
food and is continually faking his compliments to the chefs
of the world. He betrays his lack of culinary discrimination
when he orders sweet wine with his meal and then adds
artificial sweetener (Sweet 'n Low) which he carries with
him. His usual lunch is chicken and he raves about the way
it's prepared at Gino's on Lexington Avenue and 60th
Street. People joining him there who do not know about
his eating habits are often persuaded to try the same dish
and are disappointed when the main course turns out to be
perfectly ordinary roast chicken. What he doesn't finish he
takes with him, and friends are sometimes startled to see
him remove a chicken leg from his pocket at 2 A.M. and start
nibbling.

Ed Sullivan gets up around 11 A.M. and his morning starts
with a daily breakfast of one lamb chop (bought at
Gristede's), artificially sweetened pears and iced tea with
Sweet 'n Low. He does not make luncheon dates except
when he must do so for business. He normally eats lunch

alone at 3:30 or 4 P.M. at Gino's. Because of his unusual
eating hours he is never hungry when other people have
lunch. Recently he made a 1 P.M. date to dine alone with
a female reporter doing a story on him. He and Mrs.
Sullivan considered several appropriately elegant spots
and settled on La Grenouille. Ed and the reporter met there
at one o'clock, ordered drinks, talked, and at three Ed got
the check and they left. He had forgotten to order food and
the reporter was too embarrassed to tell him.

The Sullivans are night people and city people. They sold
their two-hundred-acre farm in Southbury, Connecticut,
because Ed was not temperamentally suited to country life.
They don't see much television but like to watch the Johnny
Carson show. They go to most of the theater and nightclub
openings. Friends find them a tireless couple that enjoys
staying up late, making the rounds of all the clubs and
discotheques. They will often be out until closing time at
4 A.M. and in the process wear out many of their younger
friends who have less stamina.

In the last two years they have become fans of the trotting races and go to Yonkers Raceway a few times a week.
Ed is a two-dollar bettor who plays long shots and seldom
wins. "The races start at eight o'clock. My horse starts at
eight ten." He doesn't play names or hunches but handicaps.
If he is undecided about two horses and somebody says that
one of them doesn't have a chance, that is the one he will
play.

This latest interest resulted in the Sullivans buying two
trotters last year, Verdon Hanover and Maverick Hanover.
They are in Sylvia's name and cost $13,000. Their friend
and racing partner David Granger does not expect the horses
to supplement the Sullivans' income but hopes they will

win a little. "They get tremendously excited when they bet on a horse that wins. I think the biggest thrill they could ever get is owning a winner. They'd jump through the roof of the racetrack . . . go out of their minds."

"The Sullivans are the most loving couple I've ever known," Granger says, and the opinion is shared by many people who know them well. When Sylvia leaves the table at a nightclub, Ed is liable to look at her walk away and mutter under his breath, more to himself than to any listeners, "She sure is a terrific girl." He is like any typical American husband who enjoys his marital status and urges single friends to join him. "Look at Sylvia and me. After all these years we couldn't be happier. Why don't you get married too?"

At home Ed can show a playful side. Sylvia says, "You wouldn't believe it but I never know what he's going to do next. Sometimes I'll be out shopping and when he hears my key in the door he'll hop on a couch just to yell boo."

Their life has been so quiet and free of scandal that Sylvia once playfully suggested they manufacture one. "Most important, we've never been bored. . . . Not that our marriage has been *all* sunshine and roses. When Ed first started out he had his pressures and tensions. He wasn't always the easiest man to live with." But as for now, "Ed's gay, he's attractive, he has a position to maintain and he maintains it, and he's fun to be with."

Travel is one of the things that keeps their lives exciting. They are likely to go to any spot in the world on the spur of the moment. "The more we talked about a trip," Sylvia once said, "the less chance we had of taking it. Year after year we talked about going to Nova Scotia, and we never made it. But we'd often sail for Europe on a day's notice."

On one occasion she was with a friend who remarked in the afternoon how busy Sylvia always was, traveling and so forth. "Why, you'll probably get home and find out you're going to Paris tomorrow." Mrs. Sullivan went home and found out that she *was* going to Paris tomorrow.

One of their special trips was Sullivan's first visit to Ireland. They went to Bantry Bay where his grandparents came from, and, filled with nostalgia, he told a woman serving them tea about his background: "My family came from around here."

"Indeed?"

"Yes," Sullivan said, "I'm the first of the clan to get back."

"Is that so?" said the woman. "Well, it took ye a dom long time."

In Israel their visit received a great deal of publicity because Sullivan was going to judge a contest and book the winners on his show. Mrs. Sullivan, as the wife of an American television star, was given the honor of being the official celebrity to open the country's first supermarket in Tel Aviv. She remembers that the event created a great deal of bitterness among the smaller shopkeepers—the grocers and butchers. "As a result a riot started when I cut the ribbon. They had to provide me with a police escort. I felt terrible. Like it was my fault or something."

Mrs. Sullivan, who is naturally a gracious hostess, seldom has a chance to play the role. She will never forget what happened in Russia when she did. On their last evening in Leningrad in 1959 they decided to throw a party on the roof of the Europa, the hotel where they were staying. To Sylvia's surprise, she was not allowed to charge anything. Everybody insisted on getting paid in advance and in cash.

"I had to order every single scrap beforehand. Everything
had to be counted, even to the butter pats. So I counted and
arranged and paid in advance."

Although Mrs. Sullivan had ordered an ample amount of
food and vodka, the one hundred Russians who arrived were
disposing of everything very quickly. Soon she realized the
food would not last. "It's not like you can signal the maitre d' to break out another crate of borscht. There is no such
animal as a maitre d'. . . . There are only solemn-looking officials." She went to the interpreter for help and was told the
equivalent of "I don't know from nothing. You've got to
pay." Her money was in the hotel room, not in her evening
bag. So in the middle of the party she left her guests to
get the cash, with Russians on each side to escort her. "In
front of a big picture of Khrushchev I renegotiated for just
how much more vodka and just how many olives I needed.
I paid and they marched me back upstairs."

Sylvia is so accustomed to going places on short notice
that she has frequently been written up as the woman who
can be ready in five minutes. She is asked for tips on how
to pack and what to take, and says there is one important
rule she had made for herself: "I have heard some women
who travel with their husbands say that they don't mind
wearing the same outfit day after day if they are not meeting
the same people. I am not among them; to me it is important to please Ed and to dress up for him rather than for
someone I may never meet again."

At home the Sullivans share their suite during the day
with one other person, Ed's loyal assistant, Carmine Santullo. Carmine is now in his late forties and has worked for
Sullivan since the age of sixteen. He was described in *The
New York Times* as "a gentlemanly, slight man with big

ideas." Some of them were: getting CBS stars to extend on-the-air congratulations on his boss's fifteenth anniversary; arranging for an Ed Sullivan banner to be flown across Broadway; talking twenty-two governors into proclaiming an Ed Sullivan Day and having Ed Sullivan's name sky-written.

Carmine knows Ed Sullivan so well that he, perhaps better than anyone, can anticipate the answer to a question. He can turn down requests himself, not to keep things from Sullivan, but because he knows from experience what the boss would do. He wields considerable influence but is never authoritative and, if anything, shy and self-effacing. He is a gentle, good-natured, big-hearted man who will spend the time to write a warm answer to a fan letter in his boss' name if the note happens to move him. He prefers to stay in the background and deal with people on the phone rather than in person. He never goes to the studio on Sunday but watches the show at home, where he spends most of his free time with his family. He seldom goes to the theater, nightclubs or movies, and yet he is an expert on talent and has been a help in that area over the years.

Carmine comes from a family of eight—he had five brothers and two sisters—and his father had a shoe-repair shop on 128th Street. He met Sullivan when he was a shoe-shine boy outside Loew's State Theatre in the early thirties. Ed asked if he would wait for a newspaper column and deliver it to the *News*. He said Yes and has been doing it ever since. At first he doubled as an errand boy and was then hired full-time at a salary of $35 a week. During all of his employment, he has never called his boss anything but Mr. Sullivan.

This touch of formality is just about the only thing in 1102 that isn't casual. The Sullivans live like any upper-middle class American family, which is amazing considering that almost everything in the world that can be had through money or influence is available to them.

Ed is one of the richest showmen in America. His weekly paychecks come to $4,000 before taxes, but there is additional income in other forms, such as insurance benefits and increased assets to the corporation, Sullivan Productions. His precise annual income is private information but, according to one experienced observer, "If it's less than a million dollars a year, Arnold Grant did a bad job of bargaining for him, because that's what he's worth to CBS."

He is probably television's single most influential performer. One reason is the very nature of his show. Because his format allows him to present anything, there isn't a person in the world he can't help. Private screenings of movies, special performances of plays—these are all his for the asking as well as any kind of special attention the mind can conceive.

What is remarkable is that he doesn't want it. "Daddy has never been interested in money or the things money can buy," his daughter Betty says. Even the apartment is not the lavish retreat of a man whose yearly income runs to seven figures. It is an unostentatious, nicely furnished home that could belong to countless Americans receiving a more modest salary. In fact, it was many years after Sullivan was a star before they bought their own furniture and stopped using the hotel's.

Ed and Sylvia have no domestic help of their own—no cook or butler or even maid, except the one the Hotel Delmonico provides. Sullivan walks or uses taxis rather than limousines. He kept his last Lincoln for a number of years before trading it in for his current car, a 1966 Lincoln, and he has never had a chauffeur driving it. Sylvia, the treasurer of the family, says, "We always believed that we wanted to live in such a way that we could walk away from it. We didn't want to be possessed by possessions. Ed says he doesn't want to own anything except the clothes he wears." And the only really expensive things they do own are Sylvia's fur coats and the Renoir.

"I only want what's fair for my dollar," Sullivan explains. He sees himself as an average man and that's the way he tips. He doesn't think a celebrity should leave 40 percent on a luncheon check as some stars do and resents being charged more because of his status. At the same time he is incredibly generous. Few people know that his old friend prizefighter Johnny Dundee received a weekly check from Sullivan until he died.

He is a sort of "unstar." The excessive attention and effusive flattery, which feed the egos of many performers, only make him uncomfortable. He likes plain talk and straightforwardness. He does not like being fussed over. He would rather put on his own coat than have someone help him and act subservient. Even when he had a secretary (and he doesn't anymore) he did not have her get people on the telephone for him, but dialed the numbers himself. He is one of the few performers without an agent or manager. He handles his affairs himself and Arnold Grant, his lawyer until recently, negotiated his last contract with CBS. He travels places by himself without an entourage—a show-business rarity .

It is as if the trappings of luxury—the fussing, the compliments, the limousines—could close Sullivan in just as too many appointments can do. People who submit to luxury isolate themselves from the world. Part of Ed Sullivan's success is keeping in touch with the average man. If he had a chauffeur, he'd never find out what the cabdriver thought about the comic who was on last Sunday.

Ed Sullivan's world is that of the elevator operator and not the Wall Street operator. Most of his viewers would toss aside their own drab lives in a minute to trade places with him, yet he is constantly striving to be in their shoes and stay in touch with their feelings. He is the man who has everything and wants nothing.

His career has been unique and his success spectacular, but Ed Sullivan, the man, is more unusual than either. He is one of the least predictable, most complex figures ever to dominate the national scene. This human being, who is both wise and foolish, is the least-average average man ever to conquer the imagination of the American public.

2

Boulder Dam Live on Our Stage

An 80-foot ski run and jump was constructed on the stage and skiers leaped 18 to 25 feet and did banked turns at 90 degrees on 20,000 pounds of artificial snow in the first ski show ever presented inside a television studio.

A dog played the piano and so did ten humans who performed "The Star-Spangled Banner" simultaneously under the direction of Dimitri Mitropoulos. Victor Borge played his inside a swimming pool, where Papsie Georgian did the Hawaiian hula on a paddleboard. Albert Schweitzer tuned and played the organ, tennis player Althea Gibson sang, an elephant named Little Mo water-skied and the singing Ames Brothers played a basketball game against the Harlem Globetrotters.

The only thing more unpredictable than the host has been his show.

One of the more unlikely occurrences for any program is Jackie Gleason being a flop. Sullivan explains how that happened the first time the Great One was his guest. "Everyone connected with the show thought he was a sensation, but the audience didn't go for his monologue. Jackie felt he had chosen the wrong material, so later when CBS signed him I used him again on one of the summer 'Toast' shows. He did what he wanted to, and was so great that not only did CBS find a sponsor for him but we used him on three other shows that summer."

Another failure, but a more dangerous one, was during the bow-and-arrow act of Markworth and Mayana in January, 1966. Markworth was an expert marksman who was having an off night on a live show. He was aiming at a target near Mayana's head, missing it and coming very close to the girl. The audience was tense though not completely sure this wasn't part of the act. Mayana *was* sure and needed a few stiff shots to stop shaking after the show.

Rita Hayworth also needed a few shots but before the show. Despite the fact that she was a veteran of dozens and dozens of films, she asked for and was given a double scotch to brace her for the ordeal of making her television debut.

Bette Davis did not need a bracer because she refused to appear altogether after initially saying Yes. Sullivan offered her $10,000 to do her hilarious imitation of Tallulah Bankhead, and Miss Davis flatly refused because: "Miss Bankhead isn't well enough known nationally to warrant my imitating her."

Baby Opal, a performing elephant, was another guest who didn't show up. The animal left Baltimore in a trailer driven by her trainer on Saturday around midnight in October, 1967, and was due in New York at 4 A.M. She never arrived at the studio. Someone suggested that she forgot to come, elephant's memories being what they are. Highway police combed the New Jersey Turnpike without success, and reporters called Sullivan to ask what he was

going to do. "I'm not exactly sure. We've never lost an
elephant before." Later he announced Baby Opal would
go on if the animal arrived anytime before air. This wasn't
to happen since she and her trainer had gone south from
Baltimore to a circus instead of north as the result of a
garbled communiqué from the manager in California. The
elephant turned up the following week.

Grace Kelly refused to appear . . . on a taped rebroadcast.
In June, 1963, Sullivan presented a fifteenth anniversary
show composed of highlights of his television career. One
of the segments he wanted to use was Her Serene Highness
singing "The French Lesson" from *Good News* in a duet with
Ralph Meeker. He wired her for permission to repeat the
number, as he did the other prospective guests on the show,
but Princess Grace was one of the very few to say No.

Ben Hogan's appearance came off exactly as scheduled,
although for a brief moment it didn't look like it would.
After Hogan's recovery from his near fatal automobile accident, he was in a triple tie for the United States Open
title in Philadelphia. Sullivan offered him $1,000 to appear
on the program, "win, lose or draw. I don't care how you
make out in the play-offs." Hogan couldn't commit himself for the next Sunday because the play-off might run late,
but he agreed to appear when he would be nearby in a
tournament at New Rochelle. Hogan won the play-off in
Philadelphia and Sullivan heard from a representative of
"We The People" who wanted the golfer for their Wednesday
show and were willing to give him $1,500. Sullivan says,
"At that time Hogan hadn't made the money he was to
make later. He hadn't even gotten a settlement out of the
lawsuit growing out of his accident, so I said, 'If he can
make an extra five hundred that's fine with me.'"

An hour later Hogan telephoned Sullivan to say he was turning down "We The People." He said, "They had no authority to call you. Your offer was a thousand dollars win, lose or draw. That meant more to me than any of the offers I got since I won. If you still want me for a grand, I'm not appearing on any other show."

"That is one of the classiest guys we have ever had on our show," Sullivan says.

Another athlete, Cassius Clay, came to the studio one Sunday and was his usual colorful self. He sat in the audience with his brother Rudolph, waiting to be introduced, when Maurice Chevalier came onstage. Rudolph found the face familiar but couldn't place him and asked his brother who the man was. Cassius was irritated by the stupidity of the question. "You jerk," he said, "*that* is Maurice Chev-a-leer."

It was another French singer, Jean Paul Vignon, who lived the nightmare that every guest on a live show dreads. His mind went blank. Although he was an experienced performer who had been on the show often before, he could not think of the lyrics. Sullivan calmly directed the orchestra to begin again, but Vignon remained frozen. On his third attempt he remembered the words, and when he finished he received one of the warmest ovations in the program's history.

Had Vignon been in Alan King's spot at Expo 67 there would not have been any difficulty. Like most comedians, King has the key lines of his routine printed on cue cards which stage aides flip in the appropriate places. At the dress rehearsal in Montreal King had to ignore the monologue he had prepared and go with another he knew by heart. The problem was that the boys were not turning the cue cards at the right time. The two youngsters provided by the CBC were French Canadians who couldn't understand English.

It was at Expo 67 that the police blocked off the streets to make way for the Queen of the Netherlands who was scheduled to pass. Crowds lined the sidewalks in anticipation of her arrival when Sullivan's camera crew unwittingly rode down the center going in the opposite direction. They just missed colliding with the Queen.

There was the time Allen and Rossi did a comedy routine about Boy Scouts during the dress rehearsal. Sullivan did not like the material, wanted it changed and called the comics and their writers into his dressing room. "Why don't we do the Zulu routine instead?" Marty Allen suggested. Sullivan said, "You can't do a Zulu routine. I have two hundred and fifty Zulus in the basement." And he did. This was a Sunday he was presenting a big African dance act. Allen and Rossi ended up doing the Zulu routine but changing the nationality to "Japanese."

Another foreign act that created a unique problem was the Gamelan Band from Bali. The Balinese musicians believe their drums are sacred and refused to let the stagehands touch them. They were afraid a curse would be invoked. The stagehands have a strict rule against anyone but union members moving an object on the stage but made a special concession to avoid the curse of the gods.

Another kind of reverence was accorded Carl Sandburg when he wrote and delivered a special tribute to Lincoln in February, 1962. He submitted the manuscript in advance and there was a grammatical error which was apparently a typing mistake. However, the staff hesitated to check it out for fear it had been intended as poetry.

A poet of the dance, Bolshoi prima ballerina Maya Pliset-skaya, was a guest in December, 1962. A grotesque episode occurred when she met the All-America football team who were on the same show. Miss Plisetskaya, a charming, lovely woman, was presented to the football players who expected a more conventional kind of beauty along Hollywood lines. As they met the ballerina, one of the athletes thoughtlessly said to his neighbor, "Boy, what a dog." Fortunately Miss Plisetskaya did not indicate that she heard or understood the colloquialism.

If Sullivan had been within earshot, he would have been furious, just as he was when another famous Russian, Igor Moiseyev, appeared on the show. After the Moiseyev Dancers performed for an entire hour, an incident almost marred a memorable evening. "It was the closest I ever came to losing my temper right on TV. At the end I brought Igor Moiseyev, the director, onstage for a bow. All of a sudden there was one loud boo from the balcony. I gave that man the dirtiest look that's ever been given anyplace."

Still another Russian dancer, Rudolf Nureyev, was the one person to stop the dress rehearsal, take over the program and in front of the audience calmly redirect his segment from music to camera angles. Sullivan did not offer a word of protest while the dancing star gave orders to everyone, because this was a genius and he respected talent.

There was less respect accorded Debbie Reynolds' coast hairdresser Sidney Guilaroff when he barged into the television control room to suggest appropriate camera angles for his client. He was chased out quickly. Then Debbie, not noted for her shyness, asked Ed if he would turn over his own dressing room to Guilaroff. "I never invited her back," Sullivan says.

There was an unscheduled guest whose appearance surprised everyone. In January, 1965, a man managed to enter
the studio during the live show, walk out onstage in the
middle of George Kirby's routine, say something (which no
one could understand) and leave the studio without being
caught.

Another mysterious visitor stole money from some of the
dressing rooms during one of the St. Patrick's Day programs. The guests that day included the New York City
Police Department's Emerald Society Pipe Band.

The belongings were safe but not the performers when
the Clyde Beatty tigers appeared on May 19, 1957. One of
the animals chased the veteran trainer from the caged area
and everybody in the theater froze before Beatty regained
command.

A bear provided another surprise. The animal was booked
months in advance sight unseen but after she arrived it was
discovered that she was pregnant. This may be the only
time in show business that the Act-of-God Clause has been
exercised by an animal.

A horse brought not only surprise but embarrassment.
It was the night Frankie Laine was on the program to sing
one of his record hits. The set was a western corral scene
with live horses. The stable had guaranteed that they were
housebroken, but one wasn't. "Unfortunately for Frankie
we couldn't get the animal out of camera range in time, and
the audience and the singers in the chorus began to laugh.
The song was 'I Believe.' You know how it goes: 'I believe
for every drop of rain that falls, a flower grows. . .' We closed
the curtain but you could still hear them laughing."

Another animal act that presented difficulty was Victor
Julian and his dogs. When Sullivan was in Copenhagen,

he approached Julian about coming to the United States to appear on the show. The trainer, who thought he was talking to a crank, ignored the offer and brushed off the host. Eventually Julian did appear.

Augsburg's Jungle Wonders provided a surprise ending for the appearance of the Callicoats, four singing sisters from Akron and their father. In 1963 songwriter Gladys Shelley wrote a tune, "Have A Happy Day," and to get exposure for it arranged to have the Callicoats audition for the Sullivan show singing the song. The group made a favorable impression and were booked, but when the time came to select numbers, the show asked them to do a standard from their repertoire—which Miss Shelley had not written. The decision was appealed and they were allowed two songs.

That Sunday the dress rehearsal was overlong; it was necessary to cut a tune and out went "Have A Happy Day." After the youngsters sang their standard, a monkey act named Augsburg's Jungle Wonders was introduced. Midway through the routine one of the animals went berserk and started a fight on stage with another monkey. Sullivan had the curtain closed and it looked like that was the scheduled finish. The show was now running short, so the host called on the group to sing that second tune. It was hard to tell who was more bewildered, Gladys Shelley or the trainer of the monkeys who said, "I've been looking for a good ending to that act for fifteen years."

Another unscheduled occurrence was on the 1961 Christmas Show. On December 24 Sullivan did his first complete program designed specifically for children. The audience was comprised of underprivileged boys and girls from the Metropolitan area and Sullivan had arranged to give each of the youngsters a present when the show was over. There were large boxes onstage filled with wrapped gifts, and the children lined up, walked up to the stage, shook hands with the host and received a package. There were one thousand children and at least that many gifts, but somehow several presents disappeared. By the time there were a few dozen children left it became clear that there were not enough packages to go around. It was a heartbreaking moment to see the sad faces on the remaining youngsters who were going to leave the theater empty-handed on Christmas Eve. Sullivan and his staff took down the name of every child without a present, and the gifts were delivered the next day.

The most unusual performer ever to appear has been Ed Sullivan. Although he prefers to introduce acts and get out of the way, now and then he has joined in. He danced with Gene Kelly, Carol Lawrence, and Pat Rooney, Sr.; he sang with Gary Cooper, Charles Laughton, Birgit Nilsson, Ida Lupino, Roberta Peters, Dorothy Dandridge and Peter O'Toole. He played in sketches with Lucille Ball, Gina Lollobrigida, Rita Hayworth, Bing Crosby, Red Skelton, Dan Dailey, Phil Silvers, Ernest Borgnine and Olivia de Havilland. He was a straight man for Jack Benny, Jack Carter and Rickie Layne. He joined the Kirby Stone Four and made it a quintet, and sang with Chris and Phyllis McGuire as the third McGuire sister when Dorothy could not appear because she had just had a baby.

He portrayed three Red Skelton characters, Dead Eye, Clem Kadiddlehopper and Freddie the Freeloader, in three comedy sketches on the Red Skelton show in 1961, pinch-hitting for an ailing Skelton. He was joined by Wayne and Shuster. Later he rebroadcast the Dead Eye sketch on his own show.

His most frequent performance has been with the little puppet personality, the Italian Mouse, Topo Gigio. Ed has talked with the little mouse so many times that Topo's parting words, "Hey, Eddie, keesa me good-night," have become a national catchphrase. One afternoon Sullivan was driving across the George Washington Bridge on the way to a golf match. As he approached the toll station, he heard a voice yell out his name. He looked around and saw a hand in the next vehicle rolling down the window. It belonged to a burly truck driver who leaned over and said, "Hey, Eddie, keesa me good-night."

Sullivan has opened his program by landing on the deck of an aircraft carrier in a helicopter; he has been suspended in midair by illusionist Richiardi, and has originated a show in the middle of the Hudson River. He dressed up as a clown to introduce circus acts, took a chariot ride in Rome with Charlton Heston on the set of *Ben Hur,* toured Noah's Ark with John Huston and kissed the Blarney Stone. ("You have to bend backward to do it; I almost broke my back.")

The very nature of the show has encouraged the unusual and the unexpected situation. Many of the incidents would have driven someone else off the air years ago, but Sullivan thrives on challenge. Nothing fazes him. It's all in a day's work, and no matter how bizarre the occurrence, it's merely a problem to be handled before going on to the next week, year, decade. Booking agent Mark Leddy, who has worked on the program for years, sums it up, "If Ed Sullivan fell into a sewer, he'd climb out covered with platinum."

3

The Boy Who Pumped the Church Organ

THE unpredictable world of Ed Sullivan sometimes looks like it will go on forever. However, it had a very definite beginning. Edward Vincent Sullivan was born into a family of Irishmen on September 28, 1902, in Manhattan. His parents, Peter Arthur Sullivan and Elizabeth Smith, came from Amsterdam, New York, but Peter Sullivan's father, with the unusual man's name of Florence, was born in Bantry Bay, County Cork. On his father's side there were Harringtons, Sweeneys and McNultys, and on his mother's side Drurys, Kellys, Finnans, Murphys and Gallaghers. They included two priests and one nun, lawyers, engineers, farmers, musicians, amateur painters and one newspaperman.

Ed had two brothers and four sisters, but two of the children died in infancy. One was his twin brother Daniel, who was smaller and punier and did not live past his first year. "I doubt if we were identical twins," Sullivan once said. "I've been told he was a handsome little fellow." The twin

was important to the surviving brother while he was growing up. When he was whaled by his father or switched by
the nuns at his parochial school, he would tell himself that
everything would have been different "if only Danny were
here."

His family lived on East 114th Street in an Irish and
Jewish residential area of Harlem which was beginning to
deteriorate. When Ed was five the second child died, his
sister Elizabeth, and Peter Sullivan decided to move his
family to the country where living was healthier and easier.
They went to Port Chester, New York, which Sullivan regards as his hometown.

The trip to Port Chester marked the first time that Ed
had ever seen a cow. In those days it was a sleepy little
village, with streets shaded by trees. There were horse-
drawn carriages, a village blacksmith and snake-oil salesmen. "These medicine men were my first contact with great
showmen. They had pace and authority with an audience,
the same traits I was later to enjoy in the great performers
on our television stage."

Sullivan always liked the town of Port Chester and the
people there. "They had pride in themselves. Your name or
color or religion cut no ice. You stood or fell on your own
performance."

In an earlier generation there had been prejudice. The
pastor of his church said that when the building was going
up, the people across the street pulled down their curtains and never raised them. They couldn't watch while
a Catholic church was being built. But the Port Chester of
Sullivan's childhood was a racially mixed town of Italians,
Germans, Poles and Jews and "nobody ever cared about
anyone else's race."

The family lived on the top floor of a frame, two-family house. Ed was the third oldest of the five surviving children. First in age was Helen, then Charles, Ed, his sister Mercedes and the baby, his sister Frances. The household was musical. "Somebody was always playing the piano in the parlor" or singing Victor Herbert songs, or later on playing Caruso and Melba records on the phonograph. Helen was the organist in the church of Our Lady of Mercy and Charles sang in the choir. Ed, who even as a child was not a performer, was given the job of pumping the organ. He was ten years old at the time. For pumping at low mass he received a nickel, for high mass ten cents, and once a year, for Christmas midnight mass, he was given twenty-five cents. "But there was a catch in all this; I had to put the money in the poor box." The organ was very old and it had to be pumped in a certain way so that it did not squeak. After a good deal of experience Ed became an expert and knew exactly what groove gave off the least sound. He also discovered that he could build a reservoir of air by pumping steadily, which permitted him to leave his post occasionally and go to the edge of the choir loft.

"I'll never forget one Sunday when overconfidence brought about disaster. I tripped and fell on the way back from looking at the congregation, and before I could get back to my post, the air wheezed out and the music came to a shuddering, plaintive halt. On that day I didn't get my five cents."

There was warmth and strictness in the household and the Sullivans instilled a strong sense of values in their children. They didn't have any money but "we were rich in other ways," says Helen, his oldest sister.

"Our parents taught all of us to respect the rights of all people," Sullivan says. "They taught us to respect the rights of the underdog; they taught us that all people come from God and are destined to go back to God, and they agreed that every race and creed has its shameful parts. Throughout the family, on both sides, there was a strong streak of pride and self-reliance, inspiring patriotism and a great feeling for people and a great understanding of their problems."

Peter Sullivan was a stern, brooding, moody person and, according to Ed, "the most completely fearless man I ever knew." He was the oldest son and second oldest child in a family of eight and keenly resented that he could not complete his education because, unlike his younger brothers, he had to go to work early. He was a brilliant mathematician and an outstanding debater but worked in the United States Customs House in a job which he felt frustrated his talents.

"It's unfortunate that he didn't go to college," Ed says. "Though my uncle Florence was a famous New York lawyer and my uncle Charles and my uncle Dan had been honor students at college, my father could always outreason them."

Peter Sullivan was an iron-willed man who once lost a reappointment to a New York Customs House job because he was contemptuous of the politician who appointed him and refused to send a letter of thanks for the job. "My refusal to compromise with people I despise certainly comes straight from my dad," Ed Sullivan says.

On one occasion the boys told their father that a neighbor had stolen a rooster from their yard. He stared at his growing sons in disbelief, stunned that they had not taken care of the situation themselves. He stalked out of the house, hopped the fence into the next yard, walked into the neighbor's kitchen, grabbed his rooster by both legs, and announced: "If any of you ever so much as lay a hand on anything of mine again, I'll break all of you in half."

"My mother had a wonderful and gentle personality," Sullivan says. She had a green thumb and the house and garden were always filled with flowers. She was an amateur painter and loved music and gave Ed his appreciation of the arts. Two of her happiest moments were when her children took her to see the musical *Sunny* and to listen to John Mc-Cormack sing. However, she failed in an attempt to make a musician out of Ed. "She used to give me money for piano lessons," he recalls, "but I would use it to go to the movies to see William S. Hart."

Like her husband, she was a woman of firm principles. Sullivan remembers that when he was nine years old she discovered that he and a group of friends had pocketed some candy from the corner grocery.

"She marched me back to the store and insisted I tell the entire story to Mr. Genovese, the fine old Italian gentleman who owned the place. Then she opened her purse and paid him two cents. I was so embarrassed I never stole anything again.

"As unlike as my mother and father were—she was always gay, he always stern and introspective—they had in common the most rigid sense of integrity."

The children attended St. Mary's Parochial School and then later Port Chester High. Helen was an outstanding student and was a difficult example for her brothers and sisters to follow. Ed did not get good grades and there were the inevitable comparisons. His teachers would shake their heads sadly when they returned his exams and say, "Your sister used to get a hundred."

It wasn't studies that Ed cared about. "I was interested

in sports from the minute I knew what they were all about. In any sport I was a terrific competitor. I say this without any sense of boasting because I didn't develop that spirit. It was handed down to me in the family line."

His first job was caddying for golfers at the Apawanis Club in Rye, New York. He was ten and to get there he used to walk three miles after school with his brother Charles. The pay then was thirty-five cents a round. "If you brought back a dollar to your mother you felt like a big wheel and it increased your ego," Sullivan said. He was the regular caddy for the broker Russell Colt and the first time his wife followed him around the course, "I was plenty awed." She was Ethel Barrymore. Sullivan also caddied for Nicholas Murray Butler, the educator, who was "my first great disillusion . . . a real stinker. I told that to my father. 'You'll find that all your life,' he said."

At the Apawanis Club Ed Sullivan had caddy badge 98. Badge 99 went to a youngster named Eugene Saraceni who later, as Gene Sarazen, became one of America's champion golfers. In 1922 when Sarazen won the National Open, cub reporter Sullivan proudly brought his old friend into the office and impressed the staff.

In high school Ed received ten letters for baseball (catcher), basketball (guard), football (halfback) and track (sprints), as well as a four-stitch gash on his top left eyelid against St. Peter's and a split chin.

"As an athlete Ed always came back the hero. A bit battered but always the fighter. It was indicative of things to come," Helen said.

Port Chester High was in the Westchester County League. It was "a tough league," and so he was especially proud of captaining the championship baseball team.

In the interschool competition integration was taken for granted. "When we went up into Connecticut, we ran into clubs that had Negro players. In those days this was accepted as commonplace; and so, my instinctive antagonism years later to any theory that a Negro wasn't a worthy opponent or was an inferior person. It was just as simple as that."

Sullivan's preoccupation with sports almost prevented his graduating. In those days the New York State Board of Regents insisted on a minimum of seventy-two state credits before presenting a certificate of graduation. "Edward Sullivan squeaked through with seventy-two and a half, which is drawing it as thin as possible," recalled one of Ed's teachers, the late Edward DeWitt Snow. "Ten of his credits came from Latin, in which he was notoriously poor. Luckily he sat near Bill Cigliano, who apparently took Caesar and Sullivan through Gaul."

His one good subject was English. He enjoyed reading, especially Sir Walter Scott and the adventurous tales of knights, tournaments, good and evil. "I loved the beautiful ladies and the romantic heroes."

"Through reading I came to love words and language." This aroused his desire to become a writer, which was encouraged by his mother and his sister Helen. In his senior year he became sports editor of the school paper, and he persuaded Tom Blaine, editor of the Port Chester Daily *Item,* to hire him to write up high-school sports. He was paid one dollar a column.

The twenty-six-mile train trip from Port Chester to New York was a big event, and it was in 1918 that he made the long trip to see his first Broadway stage show, *Lightnin'* starring Frank Bacon. His date was a Port Chester High

School girl, Alma Burnes. His sister Helen had to give him instructions but he did not want his date to realize that he did not know his way around New York. When they arrived at Grand Central Station he sneaked a look at the map Helen had given him. She had written next to the diagram: "Go west on 42nd Street to Broadway. Turn right and you will see the theater."

The most difficult winter of his boyhood was at the age of fifteen when Ed ran off to Chicago with sixty dollars in his pocket to enlist in the Marines. He was turned down because he did not have a birth certificate to prove his age. He wanted to make his own way and he got a job as a night worker in the Illinois Central Railroad freightyards. During one of the coldest Chicago winters on record he pushed hand trucks beginning at midnight and slept at the YMCA during the day for twenty-five cents. Later he got a job at Thompson's cafeteria as a busboy. Finally he wrote his brother Charles, told him where he was, and had him send some money for the trip home. "I thought my father would beat hell out of me, but he didn't. He just threw his arms around me and cried. It was the first time I'd ever seen my father cry."

4

Open Big and Keep It Clean

ED SULLIVAN was once asked to describe himself in a single word. "Reporter," he said.

The career which began in high school when he covered sports part-time for the Port Chester Daily *Item* became a full-time job after graduation at $10 per week. Publisher Tom Blaine hired him to cover police courts, weddings, fires, social and athletic events and the town's three funeral parlors.

"I never worked so hard before or since, but the experience was invaluable. Blaine was a hard but kindly taskmaster and he made me familiarize myself with every phase of newspaper work—not only writing and editing, but also layout, makeup and other production chores."

His first big page-one story was an interview with Babe Ruth in the lobby of the local hotel when the Yankee star was in town for an exhibition game.

Another important assignment was covering a baseball game between the Philadelphia Athletics and a semipro team from the Russell Birdsall and Ward Bolt and Nut Company. RB&W, as they called it, was important to the

Port Chester economy, so "all hell broke loose" when Sullivan wrote that the Athletics made a laughing stock of the game by using a third-string pitcher. One of Ward's key men phoned Blaine and demanded an apology from the reporter in the next day's paper. Sullivan refused, saying he had written the truth from his own knowledge as a player. "Mr. Blaine looked at me over his glasses, pulled the pipe out of his mouth and said, 'Oh you Irish!'" Blaine relayed Sullivan's feelings over the telephone and was surprised by the response: "Good for him. Tell him always to stick to his guns if he's right." But the caller now suggested that Sullivan was biased since he was the catcher for another local team, the semipro Saxer Catholic Club. Sullivan not only made a strong defense of his impartiality but insisted that Saxer could beat RB&W. The result was a "blood game" which Saxer won two to one.

Sullivan's work on the *Item* earned him a raise to twelve dollars a week and the title of sports editor, but he was restless and eager to improve himself. He heard there was a job open in the sports department of the Hartford *Post,* applied for it in person and was hired on the spot for $50 a week. His mother and sister Helen were excited by the opportunity and considered it a step to bigger things. His father thought he should build a future for himself in Port Chester but said he would not stand in the way.

Ed departed with great fanfare. "Port Chester gave me a big going-away party, speeches, a watch, the whole works."

One week after Ed arrived at the Hartford *Post* the owner, Connecticut Representative Spellacy, announced that the paper would be sold. Everyone was given two weeks' salary and was out of a job. Sullivan's pride would not permit him to go home a failure, and he decided to hide the folding of the paper from his family. He took a job wrapping bundles in the basement of a Hartford department store and planned to carry on the deception for at least two weeks by bringing home his severance pay on weekends and pretending it was his salary. "Every night when I came back from the store, I would pray before going to sleep. I had great faith in the rosary, and I never prayed so hard or with such implicit belief."

He only had to conceal his situation for seven days, because with fortunate timing he heard from the New York Evening *Mail*. Earlier Jack Lawrence, a fellow alumnus of the *Item* who went to the *Mail*, had given Sullivan letters of introduction to the paper. Now there was an opening for a man who could write scholastic sports. Sullivan was hired to work for the school-page editor, Jack Jackowitz, and to cover DeWitt Clinton, Morris, Commerce and other New York high schools.

Triumphantly Sullivan returned to Port Chester to tell everyone about his big promotion.

"I am so happy!" his mother said. "When I read in the paper last week that the Hartford *Post* had been sold, I thought sure you'd be back on the *Item*."

At the Port Chester and Hartford papers Sullivan had written all his copy in longhand. When he did the same thing at the Evening *Mail* there were loud protests from the composing room, and Jackowitz insisted that he learn to type. Every day he went to the paper's small morgue, sat down at an empty typewriter and copied editorials from *The New York Times*. After months of practice he was good enough to get by with two fingers, hunt and peck.

When Hugh S. Fullerton became the new sports editor of the paper, Sullivan was promoted into the regular sports department and made college-sports editor, with golf and tennis as sidelines.

In his new assignment he tried to write in a sophisticated style and fell flat on his face. His superior suggested that perhaps he was not cut out for newspaper work.

"I was pressing and getting worse day by day. Like most youngsters in any field who come to New York, I tried to copy what I assumed to be the New York style instead of writing the way I did at the *Item*.

"One day Fullerton's assistant, Larry Jacobs, assigned me to cover a dog show, and I figured that was the end. I had never been to a dog show and didn't know one breed from another." He was angry because he assumed his boss was trying to make him look foolish. While he was at the show he saw a little girl looking at an English bulldog. She turned to her mother and asked, "How do they wash their faces with all those wrinkles?" The remark inspired him and he let his imagination go. He wrote the article as if he were answering a child's questions about the dogs.

On the train back home to Port Chester that night he had second thoughts about the way he had treated his assignment and tried to figure out how to pull back his copy.

"As the night wore on, I became more and more terrified as I imagined what the sophisticated New York sports-writers would think when they picked up this piece of whimsy."

On his way in to the office the next day he was certain he was out of a job. Then he picked up a copy of the Evening *Mail*.

"I damn near dropped dead because there was my story with a two-column head on it and my by-line spread across two columns. Completely dazed, I didn't take the downtown train. I got on the shuttle train to Times Square and rode back and forth from Grand Central to Times Square at least five round trips, reading and rereading the story of the little girl. At times I was tempted to nudge the passenger next to me and tell him 'I'm Ed Sullivan.' "

The story launched him as a top professional newspaperman and taught him a lesson he never forgot. In finding success by using the style which came naturally to him, "I learned that the important thing is to be yourself."

The Evening *Mail* was staffed by some of the top newspapermen in the business including Rube Goldberg, Mary Margaret McBride, Russell Crouse, and Robert Ripley. The competition was keen but Sullivan was "determined to be the best sportswriter in New York."

His first big story was an interview with Jack Dempsey in 1923 at the Alamac Hotel. Sullivan was overwhelmed by the prospect of meeting his idol. "When I knocked at Dempsey's door, he opened it himself—and I remember how big he looked. He seemed to fill the doorway. He was wearing a loud striped bathrobe and he was smiling." He invited Sullivan to join him for breakfast, which he had ordered in advance. The grapefruit on the table was in a bowl of ice and Sullivan said it was the first time he had ever seen it served that way. Dempsey smiled and said, "When I was a kid I never saw a grapefruit." The article was a success because Sullivan uncovered a new angle: for years sportswriters had incorrectly stated Dempsey started fighting in 1913 when it was actually five years earlier.

His best remembered assignment at the *Mail* was covering a tennis match. In writing up the article he referred to California tennis champion Helen Wills as "little poker face," a nickname that was to stay with her afterward. During the 1950's Sullivan sent Helen Wills a letter of congratulations on her birthday and reintroduced himself as the tennis writer who had given her the nickname. He commented on the irony of these words coming back to haunt him since the same phrase was being used to describe his manner as a television host. "She sent me back a charming note."

Sullivan was enthusiastic about his job at the *Mail* and the colorful sporting personalities he met. "The door opened to a world more glamorous, fascinating and exciting than I'd ever imagined, for at the time the country was just entering what might be called the golden age of sports." Names like Ruth, Hornsby, Dempsey and Tilden became legends. Ice skating star Joe Moore and the late featherweight champion Johnny Dundee were to be his close personal friends, and Moore still is today. Sullivan's salary was $75 a week and he used it to have fun. He bought himself a car, a Durant, and wore hand-tailored suits and custom-made shirts. He had a girl in Port Chester whom he took out on weekends, and soon he was seen around town in the company of a succession of extravagantly pretty flappers. He lived over Duffy's Tavern on West 48th Street and spent evenings at the brassy nightclubs of the period. He was frequently mistaken for a rising young actor named Humphrey Bogart, who also had high cheekbones and a deadpan expression.

"It was very exciting in those days. It was the first time I'd seen big nightclub shows and all the top people. And it was a pretty rough citizenry inhabiting the town at the time."

His favorite spot was the Silver Slipper on West 48th Street where he went almost every evening. "Ruby Keeler used to be on the bill and Van and Schenck and Clayton, Jackson and Durante. Lou Clayton and I would sit up all night and then go out to Flushing for a round of golf first thing in the morning. We'd pick up a milkman for caddy."

In the winter of 1924 the editor of the *Mail* sent him to Florida to cover the winter-season sports. The good times continued there but ended abruptly when the *Mail* was purchased by the *Sun* and the new publisher decided to scrap the paper. Sullivan was stranded in Florida without a job or savings. Golf star Tommy Armour lent him $50 and suggested he see Grantland Rice, who was in Miami at the time. Rice advised him to take interim work until he could save some money, and Rice and Ray McCarthy got him a job as publicist at the golf course at Ormond Beach at $50 a week plus room and board. He booked exhibition matches and arranged stunts and tournaments and picked up a few extra dollars as resident correspondent for Associated Press and United Press.

Soon after he arrived, a big sports story came his way. Multimillionaire banker George D. Baker was coming to Ormond Beach to play a golf match with the aging John D. Rockefeller, Sr., who made his winter home there. Sullivan wired the big Metropolitan papers to find out if they wanted sports copy about two of the world's wealthiest men, and they were all interested.

After the eight-hole match was finished, Sullivan wrote up his dispatch, but Johnson, the manager of the Hotel Ormond, did not want it sent. "If I were a young man," he said, "I would hesitate to offend two men who are important in the life of the country." Sullivan then suggested that the hotel ingratiate itself with the influential newcomers by putting its services at their disposal. They had traveled by private railroad car and might be without kitchen facilities. Johnson liked the idea and let Sullivan extend the courtesy in person. The young reporter went to the siding where he met Loomis, whose railroad had supplied the private car. He introduced himself, made the offer which was appreciated but turned down. Sullivan then asked Loomis to look over his dispatch to make certain it contained nothing objectionable. Loomis approved and on request initialed the copy which the reporter then brought back to Johnson. He filed the story and it became front-page news around the country. He made about $235. Two days later he received "a very human note" from John D. Rockefeller who said that although Baker had beaten him hole by hole, Rockefeller had won in total strokes. Sullivan always regretted not saving that letter.

Years later when he was an established television star and staying in Florida he picked up a publication called "Southern Golfer" one day and in it saw a one-column advertisement for the Hotel Ormond and its golf course. It said "visit the course where John D. Rockefeller and Ed Sullivan once played."

The job situation was not good in New York so, after the winter, Sullivan settled for a position as sportswriter with the Philadelphia *Ledger* at $35 a week. From there he moved to New York and a series of short-lived jobs writing sports at the Morning *World*, under George Daley, whom he called a "perfectionist," at the New York *Bulletin* and at the *Leader*, published by Norman Thomas. For two years he worked on the Morning *Telegraph* until 1927 when Will Gould, sports cartoonist at Bernarr Macfadden's New York *Graphic*, suggested that he move over there and do articles for the Saturday sports-magazine insert which they were

adding to the paper. Sullivan joined the *Graphic* and later
became sports editor through the unusual method of elec-
tion by the sportswriters.

It was here that he had his first opportunity to make a
strong protest in print on behalf of the Negro. Before a
scheduled football game between N.Y.U. and the University
of Georgia he found out that the contract between the two
schools included a clause in which N.Y.U. agreed to bench
a Negro player for the entire game.

"I was sickened. For the next week I castigated New York
University's immorality and suggested that their Hall of
Fame be torn down and transferred to some other university
with a higher regard for a boy's dignity."

The *Graphic*, a tabloid, was one of the brassiest scandal
sheets in New York and Sullivan himself later called it
"a step removed from pornography." However, some of
America's foremost newsmen worked there, including Walter Winchell, who covered Broadway, and Louis Sobol, assigned to entertainment. Bernarr Macfadden, who ran the
paper, was a zany eccentric who wanted the same success as
a newspaper publisher that he had achieved with physical-
culture magazines. His managing editor was Emil Gauvreau
who battled furiously with Winchell. Sullivan's feelings toward the columnist were scarcely any warmer. From the beginning he found the man irritating and was particularly
delighted when his friend Lou Clayton told him Winchell
never played the Palace, as he had bragged. According to
Clayton, Winchell was a small-timer and waved an American flag as he exited to get applause. Sullivan later described
Winchell by saying, "as in vaudeville, he always was one to
wave an American flag."

Winchell's column, "Broadway Hearsay," was popular

and William Randolph Hearst, Sr., lured him away to the Daily *Mirror*. Louis Sobol replaced Winchell as the *Graphic* columnist until Hearst grabbed Sobol too for his *Journal-American*. Sullivan was then given the Broadway column.

"I didn't want the job, but it was either take it or be fired. I took it but determined never to rap anyone the way some columnists did. I don't think I have the right to pass final judgment on other people's behavior."

The first column, "Ed Sullivan Sees Broadway," appeared on June 1, 1931. It was an angry sermon which created a stir at the time and has often been quoted since.

He wrote:

> I charge the Broadway columnists with defaming the street. I have entered a field of writing that ranks so low that it is difficult to distinguish any one columnist from his road companions. I have entered a field which offers scant competition. The Broadway columnists have lifted themselves to distinction by borrowed gags, gossip that is not always kindly and keyholes that too often reveal what might better be hidden. Phonies will receive no comfort in this space. To get into this particular column will be a badge of merit and a citation—divorces will not be propagated in this column. ... In my capacity as drama critic I pledge you of the theater that if I like the show I will say so without any ambiguities of phrasing that might protect my *Variety* box score. ... With the theater in the doldrums, it means a decisive voice and I promise to supply it.

The reaction varied from uncertainty to hilarity. Winchell considered it a personal attack and was furious. Macfadden wondered if his new reporter was serious and was told by an editor it didn't matter because no Broadway column could be written that way for a week. Sullivan explained later that he "tried to write a big send-off, a column that you wouldn't be ashamed to take home and show the children." Observers have noted that today he still follows the philosophy underlying his initial column: "Open big and keep it clean."

His detractors have enjoyed picking out early items which were exceptions to his rules.

June 25, 1931. "Grover Cleveland Alexander is back with his wife and off the booze."

July 17, 1931. "Everyone who played a lead in *The Marriage Circle,* including Lubitsch, the director, has been divorced."

August 8, 1931. "Abe Lyman's sister is returning from the coast ... without her hubby."

August 13, 1931. "Jean Malin belted a heckler last night at one of the local clubs.... All that twitters isn't pansy...."

Sullivan joined the ranks and became his own critic by reminding people of his opening-night review of August Strindberg's *The Father.* He did not like the show and said so. "I remember telling the author he ought to rewrite the entire second act. It wasn't until the next day that I found out that Strindberg was dead."

On January 22, 1932, Sullivan reviewed himself and how well he had stuck to his credo: "Just twice in eight months of Broadway columning have I linked a married man with a girl, both times through sheer ignorance of the tie that binds, and both times to my complete embarrassment when I learned of my blunders." Later that same year the New York *Graphic* folded. One obituary said: "The *Graphic,* which anticipated every news event except its own demise, died."

One week before the *Graphic* closed shop Sullivan got a phone call from Captain Joe Patterson of the *News* who offered him a job and told him to come over and talk. Sullivan feared it was a crank call and phoned back the secretary to make certain. He was hired at a salary of $200 a week, $175 a week less than he was making at the *Graphic,* but the loss of income was softened by his CBS radio show for American Safety Razor which was bringing him $1,000 a week.

In his first year at the *News* he received just one memo from Patterson. It dealt with a column he wrote about Samuel Goldwyn's "newest discovery" Anna Sten, who had a big advertising and publicity investment behind her. Sullivan wrote that Anna Sten bored him and the next day the Patterson memo was on his desk. "I do not say that I disagree with your opinion. However, I am deeply disturbed that any writer of mine would recklessly jeopardize the professional career of a young actress." Sullivan was impressed by the note. "I read the memo and reread it. And as the meaning sunk in, I thought to myself: here indeed is a great man." He presumed Patterson's concern was for the young actress and not advertising revenue.

Three years to the day after he wrote his first Broadway column for the *Graphic,* he summed up his accomplishments: "Just how well I've lived up to my promises of 1931 is difficult to tell. . . . My platform against gossip hasn't a single plank left in it, for in the course of a week I run two full gossip columns. The reason I do it is because the readers demand it."

Sullivan has written for the *News* continuously since 1932. In November, 1940, he seriously considered a job offer from Billy Wilkerson, publisher of the Hollywood *Reporter.*

Captain Patterson was on a fishing trip with his wife Mary and Sullivan wired him. The answering telegram was:

If you can better yourself permanently, I would not wish to stand in your way. Mary suggests your health might be involved and that, of course, is a matter you know best. But I want to make it clear I consider you one of our best men and that, *rebus sic stanibus,* you can stay with us as long as you want.

J. M. Patterson

The date was November 16, 1940.

"Whenever I felt low, I dug out that wire," Sullivan said later.

He has been based in New York for his entire career except for the Hollywood years from 1937 to 1940. When he went to California, the *News* wanted their coast columnist, Sidney Skolsky, to change places with him. Skolsky issued a formal statement to the press: "The *News* wanted me to return to do a Broadway column. I believe that Broadway columns are as passé as Broadway. Therefore I have resigned." The obituary for Broadway was as premature as the one for Mark Twain which caused the author to comment: "The report of my death has been grossly exaggerated."

Sullivan's column has been criticized as frequently as his television show. People who like it call it warm, personal and human, and those who don't use adjectives such as, mundane, corny, gossipy and preachy.

"Open big and keep it clean" was always the guideline. He considers the lead the crucial sentence in his copy and he is as bothered by malicious gossip today as in 1931. He claims that he's never written a mean column he hasn't regretted. Recently he ran an item about the marital problems of a well-known ballplayer whom he mentioned by name. The athlete, a friend, was hurt and telephoned. "Ed, why did you do that?" Sullivan couldn't find an appropriate answer. When he hung up the phone, he turned to his wife. "Sylvia, why did I do that?"

Pre-television columns come back to haunt him now such as the one in which he said, "There ought to be a law against introduction of celebs in theaters and nightclubs, for it is a nuisance at best. The master of ceremonies always winds up with a crop of new enemies, through overlooking somebody or other."

He would probably like to forget writing that Will Rogers' brand of humor has "too much bite and bitterness to suit me. . . . Rogers never has been able to discriminate between wit and personalities." Rogers replied: "I know that mine is not exactly the type of humor (if you can call it that) that has appealed to you younger boys who have Broadway at your feet. But us country columnists, they don't expect much from us."

Today Ed Sullivan's salary as a newspaperman is less than $200 a week. This is barely enough for the column to pay its own way but still it appears in a paper with two-million circulation, largest in the United States. He does two columns a week, which appear on Monday and Friday, and puts them together on Thursday between twelve thirty and two thirty and on Sunday before his one o'clock dress rehearsal. "I write the column in two hours and forty seven years," he says, but the hourly estimate is conservative. He will finish it to his own satisfaction, even if that means spending more than the allotted two hours and showing up late for Sunday dress rehearsal.

He takes pride in writing his own copy and enjoys the

opportunity to speak out on subjects that he can't discuss on television. He is always looking for material, and he finds it everywhere, whether it's on a plane talking to the stewardess and pilot or in a photo studio chatting with the photographer's assistant.

Ed Sullivan used to be one of America's most popular columnists, and he is the one man to equal his newspaper success in electronic journalism. To some extent he achieved the transition by maintaining his values, by concerning himself with news value and pacing, by opening big and keeping it clean.

Now the age of the column is over, and his influence no longer derives from the print medium. At thirty seconds after eight o'clock on Sunday nights announcer Ralph Paul says, ". . . and here he is, live from New York, Ed Sullivan." In those few seconds there is a weekly epitaph to another era. It does not lie in the spoken words but in the ones that are no longer heard. There was a time when the introduction was, "and here he is, the syndicated columnist of the *Daily News*, Ed Sullivan."

5

The Women in His Life

In 1926 Sylvia Weinstein celebrated her graduation from high school at the Casa Lopez nightclub in New York where the strolling violinist was a man named Xavier Cugat. Sitting at the next table was a wiry young Irishman from Port Chester, New York, who was sports editor of the New York *Graphic*, Ed Sullivan. Ed went to the Casa Lopez frequently. It was the first time Sylvia had ever been in a nightclub.

During the evening some of the people at Sullivan's table waved hello to the crowd at the next table. "I looked over and was attracted by a very stunning brunette youngster." He asked Joe Russell, publicity man for the club, to introduce him and he met Sylvia Weinstein.

Sullivan sat down at her table, said that Suzanne Lenglen was playing tennis at Madison Square Garden a few days later and asked if she liked tennis. "Of course I said I loved it. Ed was very attractive."

Sullivan talked about boxing and she loved that too. Before the evening was over he asked her for two dates. Would she like to see the Wills-Sharkey prizefight at Ebbets Field next week? And how about watching Suzanne Lenglen play tennis a few days later? Sylvia accepted and this was the beginning of a three-and-a-half-year romance.

The courtship was tempestuous and they broke up numerous times. Sylvia says that they were always having farewell dinner parties. "Afterward we would say, 'Meet you for another good-bye party in two weeks.'" Sullivan would tell her that a marriage wouldn't work out and they would separate after a Monday date. By Thursday Sullivan would call and say, "I can't stand it anymore." And the following Sunday he would say, "This is the end."

"Ed had no intention of getting married," Sylvia says, "but finally I trapped him into eloping." Sullivan says that at the time "there wasn't what I'd call resentment by our families, but there was apprehension." Sylvia describes Ed's family as "all devout Catholics—who were opposed to the marriage."

Sylvia was the daughter of Julius Weinstein, a wealthy New York real-estate man. She calls her Jewish background "the regular Marjorie Morningstar world of the time. If I had married a manufacturer I would probably have become a typical Shirley." Her family was not religious but they went to temple on the high holy days.

When she finally got around to telling her family that she was going steady, she said it was with Ed Solomon. When she told her brother Ed was a sportswriter for the *Graphic,* he said, "Oh, you mean Ed Sullivan, not Solomon." Her family did not object strongly to the religious differences. They knew she was deeply involved emotionally and wanted her to be happy.

The marriage was supposed to be a secret. They met at City Hall and the witnesses were Sylvia's friend Ruth

Sanburg and Ed's friends Jim Kahn, ex-sportswriter, and Johnny Dundee. The couple was assured that the marriage would not be made public until Ed gave his okay. This would be after the Roman Catholic wedding service was performed by the Reverend Father Joseph Connors of West Orange, New Jersey, on Thursday night and they spent a two-day honeymoon in Atlantic City the following weekend. Then they would tell their parents.

The secrecy did not last long. They had dinner with Dundee at the Roosevelt Hotel and when they returned to Sullivan's apartment they discovered City Hall hadn't concealed the marriage. Reporters were phoning and a photographer was waiting. They called up their families right away to tell them before they read about it in the newspapers. A few days later the Catholic ceremony was performed as planned.

They had an agreement that the children would be brought up as Catholic, and Sylvia taught Betty her catechism and sent her off to mass and the sacraments. "Mother was never a practicing Jew," Betty says, "but she never thought of becoming a Catholic."

For the first seven years of Betty's life the family lived in apartment houses. From 1937 to 1940, when Sullivan wrote his column from Hollywood, the trio lived in Beverly Hills in a house complete with garden. But in 1940 Sullivan returned to New York and the family moved into the Astor, the beginning of their hotel life.

A childhood friend of Betty's describes the days in the Astor Hotel as "the life of a kind of Broadway Eloise ... a steady stream of room service and a movie a night on free passes." At that time Betty was attending Marymount Grammar School. She ate most of her meals with a paid

companion across the street from the hotel at Child's restaurant, which she preferred to the more elegant places like
the Colony or Le Pavillon "because they like me for me at
Child's, not because I'm your daughter."

In 1944 when Betty was fourteen they moved to the
twenty-second floor of the Delmonico. Then she ate dinner
with her parents and they went to a different restaurant
every night. Hotel life and restaurant dinners showed
Betty a great deal of glamorous New York, but one of
the things she missed was holiday meals with the family
all together. "At fourteen I felt penned up in New York. A
home to me is wall-to-wall carpeting and holiday dinners."

Today Betty has a different kind of life as the wife of
Bob Precht, producer of "The Ed Sullivan Show," and
mother of five children. They live in a house in Scarsdale
where they have wall-to-wall carpeting and family dinners.

As Betty grew up the three Sullivans were a close family
unit. "Sylvia and I agreed that we must treat our young
daughter with the dignity of an adult. We listened to what
she had to say and we never broke a promise to her."

Sullivan was not a demonstrative parent ("A cheek-to-
cheek kiss and a brief hug is overdoing it as far as daddy
is concerned"), but no father was ever more adoring. "Ed
might lose his temper with everyone in the world, and
perhaps he did, but never with Betty," says a friend who
has known them for years.

Sullivan once described his daughter as "an exceptional
little girl, possessed of great poise, tact and an instinctive
sympathy for people."

Ed used to help Betty with her schoolwork, and he once
wrote skits for her school musical comedy. Milton Berle
did lyrics for the songs. Whenever Betty was worried

about something like a school examination, her father would
leave a note for her on the hall table. She would see it in
the morning while he was still asleep and read it on the way
to school. It usually said something like "Read the questions
carefully, then take a deep breath and relax." They always
ended the same way: "Win, lose or draw—we love you,
Daddy."

When Betty graduated from U.C.L.A. in 1952 her parents gave her a leather-bound book that told her "life's
story." In it were her childhood pictures and all the notes
her father had written her which she had saved. The title
was embossed in gold on the cover: "Win, Lose or Draw
... Limited Edition. Love, Unlimited." The first note in
the book was dated late in 1939 and written on Astor Hotel
stationery:

> Betty Dear—
> Your nice note was the best thing I've ever found on my
> pillow. Probably at times I demand too much perfection
> from a little girl who is only nine years old, but I do mean
> well and I guess I expect a high standard from you because
> I love you so much.
> My nerves have been a little bit bouncy lately, and little
> things have annoyed me as much as bigger things. So I'll
> match your sweetness in saying that you were sorry by say-
> ing in turn that I'm sorry too that I spoiled your evening
> and your mommy's evening. At least Mommy got even by
> beating me soundly at cards.
> This really should be the most splendid month of the en-
> tire year—Mommy's birthday, your birthday and Christmas
> all together—so let's you and I make an agreement that
> we'll never again raise our voices or wrinkle our faces, be-
> cause in this cold weather our faces might get frozen into
> those expressions and that would be terrible.
>
>   Affectionately, Daddy

The last entry bore the date of Betty Sullivan's wedding: June 27, 1952:

> Betty Dearest:
>
> This is the most wonderful day in your lives and the life of your mother and me. You are two fine kids, your love is based on mutual respect for each other's rights, and it will be a happy marriage.
>
> I'm not going to make this a long letter.
>
> Our deep love for you now reaches out to embrace Bob.
>
> And don't worry about your mother, because I'll redouble my affection for her so that, in these early months, she won't miss you.
>
> God love you both and protect you and grant you just as much happiness as He has granted your mother and daddy.
>
> > With all my love,
> > Daddy

The family is still close and they are all practical people with a streak of sentimentality. Everywhere Sullivan goes he carries a St. Christopher medal, a present from the women in his life. The medal has a little companion circular piece with an inscription: "St. Christopher protect him because we love him very much, Sylvia and Betty."

Protection is what he needed on August 6, 1956, when he was driving his automobile and rounded a curve on Route 8 in Seymour, Connecticut. "The kid in the other car was an X-ray technician. He'd been working late at night at a hospital and evidently he fell asleep at the wheel as he made his turn. I was driving and I saw him come at us head-on. It's one of the few times that there's been a head-on collision in which people haven't been killed."

It was after midnight on Sunday and Sullivan and Bob Precht were returning to the farm in Southbury which the

Sullivans owned at that time. They were driving from Bridgeport, where they had flown in an Army plane from McGuire Air Force Base in New Jersey, site of that evening's show. Sullivan was thrown from the car.

"The next thing I knew, I was stretched out by the side of a country road on a piece of tarpaulin. There was the taste of blood in my mouth and I could hardly breathe because it felt as though my entire chest had been caved in. I heard police whistles, as though they were far away, and I thought to myself dully: So this is it.

"A man with a flashlight threw a beam full in my face. 'Hey, Doc, come here quick. He's Ed Sullivan.' Even in my agony I enjoyed the doctor's reply. 'I don't know who he is. After an automobile smashup they all look alike.' "

Sullivan fractured his breastbone and seven ribs and his entire chest was caved in. (He was off the show for five weeks and Phil Silvers, Red Skelton, Kirk Douglas, Patti Page and Charles Laughton substituted as hosts.) Precht had facial abrasions and a broken shin bone. There were no serious injuries to the other driver or to their one passenger, Ralph Cacace, night watchman of their farm which they sold after the accident. All four were taken in an ambulance to the hospital in Derby.

"An hour or so later when Sylvia and Betty came into the hospital room where Bob and I were stretched out in beds, their faces were chalk-white, their eyes were shocked, but they were smiling. As Sylvia leaned down to kiss me she whispered, 'Everything's going to be all right, darling. And don't forget, win, lose, or draw, I love you.' "

People call Ed and Sylvia "an average couple," and they even argue like average couples. "Ed has a terrific temper. He asks me to hand him his glasses, or some small thing,

and if I don't do it promptly he gets the glasses and one
word leads to another. Once the fight starts, he's very good
at remembering all the little things I didn't do for him two
years ago."

Sullivan says his wife gave up golf because "I drove her
nuts correcting her backswing."

Sylvia is a realist. "People say I know how to handle
him. Of course he has a temper and can be unreasonable.
I may say, 'It's a nice day,' and if he's annoyed at something he will say, 'Why?' or some such silly thing. Having
a temper and problems on his mind, Ed has to find someone to let it out on. It may be on me, but I can honestly
say it doesn't happen very often, and I'm no saint either.
I don't mind taking it because everyone has to have someone they can relax with and be natural with. In all our
life together we have never had an important fight. I do
think Ed is very much in love with me."

Underlying the superficial frictions of everyday marriage
is a deep mutual respect and affection that has withstood
the test of time. Sullivan does not find it easy to express
emotions, but he once described his feelings for his wife
with a simplicity and sincerity bordering on eloquence.

"Sylvia just lets me alone when I'm in a mood, and she's
been following that system during our entire married life.
She knows me, but good. Sylvia has a wonderful disposition, a great sense of humor. In fact she's wonderful in
every way. She'd have to be because I imagine I'm difficult
to get along with at times. Sylvia is a great rooting section
for me. More than once she has believed in me enough to
stand behind me on a gamble. Several times I've been faced
with a decision to risk temporary security, to take a chance
on a job offer that was anything but secure. She has always

felt that what I wanted to do was the only consideration. If it hadn't been for her, I'm sure I wouldn't be where I am now. She has always been the silent and powerful chorus in the background. Hers has been the grim and the lonely job of waiting and watching; no matter what I've done, she's been there."

6

Everyone Needed a Second Job

"Newspaper wages were among the worst and everyone needed a second job."

This is how Ed Sullivan explains his entry into show
business.

It began in the late 1920's when he was sports editor of
the Evening *Graphic*. Newsmen of the period occasionally
acted as master of ceremonies at sports banquets and benefit
shows. Sullivan originated and hosted the *Graphic* All-
Sports Dinner which was so successful that it became an
annual event. When Winchell left the paper, Sullivan took
over booking the entertainment as well as the sports talent.

This led to a radio program in 1930 for Adam Hats and
then the radio hosting job for the Gerardine program at
$1,000 a week. About fifteen different personalities were
considered, but Sullivan was chosen because of his impressive audition program. George M. Cohan, who had
never been on radio before, went to the studio with Sullivan
and described the evening his song "Over There" was performed in public for the first time. It was at a patriotic
World War I rally in Baltimore which President Wilson
was scheduled to attend. During the show the lights went

out and people became tense because of rumors that German spies were going to blow up the building. Gus Edwards came onstage to calm the audience, remembered the lyrics to "Over There," which he had heard only once, and sang to prevent a panic. The only lighting came from the headlights of automobiles parked outside the armory.

In 1932 Sullivan came to CBS with a program entitled "Broadway's Greatest Thrills" and later "Ed Sullivan Entertains," which originated at the famed 21 Club in New York. Said one review: "The clackety-clack of the Remington, with the carriage moved back intermittently, is a switch on the Winchellian telegraphic staccato.... Although Sullivan's voice does not have the weight and authority for this type of work, it's no drawback. Different type pipes are welcome." He introduced many popular personalities to the medium including Jimmy Durante, Irving Berlin, Florenz Ziegfeld, Jack Pearl and Frances Langford. On March 29, 1932, a comedian made his broadcasting debut reluctantly because he "didn't know anything about radio." He was Jack Benny. On his tenth anniversary on the air in 1942 Benny repeated the script of that first broadcast on his own program.

Although Sullivan presented an impressive roster of celebrities, he did not set any longevity records. "I would put together a radio program and get it on the air. Everybody would tell me how good it was, but after a few weeks it would be dropped."

His radio work led to his first job as master of ceremonies after becoming a Broadway columnist. It was at the one-hundred-dollar-a-plate dinner of the radio division of the United Jewish Federation at the Hotel Plaza in 1932. Afterward, in April, 1932, he received a call from Boris Morros of the Paramount Theatre who offered him $1,000 a week to put on a variety show there. "You must be crazy," Sullivan said, stunned and pleased by the offer. Morros thought Sullivan was bargaining. "I'll make it fifteen hundred dollars," he said. "You're still crazy," Sullivan replied. By the end of the day the offer was up to $3,750. "By then I knew that if I didn't take it, I was the one who was crazy." Sullivan named his review "Gems of the Town." It played with a film called *Take a Chance*.

Time magazine wrote: "Though at war with Winchell, Ed, like a good general, learned a great deal from his enemy. Winchell emceed a stage show at Manhattan's Paramount, using the pressure of his column to line up good acts at a nominal cost. Ed did the same and earned $3,750 for a week's stand."

A succession of stage shows at Loew's State Theatre followed. At first Harry Rose, "the Broadway Jester," was billed as master of ceremonies. One of the earliest shows starred Rose, Eleanor Powell and Eddie Peabody, Mackey and Lavelle, Cackles O'Neil, Gene Marvey, the Tic-Toc Girls and the music of Ruby Zwerling and the Loew's State Senators. Even then Sullivan was introducing celebrities in the audience and being criticized in the press for his manner as a host. *Variety* wrote:

> Harry Rose with his aggressive style of emceeing is working hard this week and looks responsible for keeping the show together.... His sustained clicking makes it easier for the rest of the troupe, especially for Sullivan who found Rose's help quite handy in the microphone moments.... As at the Paramount, Sullivan is tossing in visiting celebs at each show. At the performance viewed here he brought on Abner Silver, the songwriter, and Tony Canzoneri, ex-lightweight champ.

The "Dawn Patrol" revues, as they came to be called, reappeared frequently at Loew's State on the same bill with such films as *Operator Thirteen*, with Marion Davies, *The Whole Town's Talking*, with Edward G. Robinson, and *Broadway Gondolier*, with Joan Blondell and Dick Powell. Critics applauded Sullivan for "delivering a good show."

On July 6, 1934, he presented "The All-Star All-American Nightclub Review of 1934" with Mr. and Mrs. Paul Mears, ballroom dancers, Georgie Tapps, Barbara Blane, Ken Harvey and singer Joan Abbott, who today is one of the Sullivans' closest friends along with her husband Benny Gaines.

While presenting the Loew's State variety shows, he was still writing six columns a week. "Thank Heaven I was married. If I'd tried to do all that work and still cover 3 A.M. nightclub shows the way I'd done when I was on the *Mail*, I'd have been a nervous wreck."

One of Sullivan's memorable offstage moments at Loew's State Theatre took place when Broadway producer A. C. Blumenthal brought a friend backstage to his dressing room to meet him between shows. Sullivan was brusque to the visitor because he was working against a deadline to complete a column. When he finished he spoke to the guest. "Excuse me, but I didn't get your name."

"Wells," the man answered in an English accent.

"Oh, just like the English writer," Sullivan replied.

"You dope," said Blumenthal, "he *is* H. G. Wells." Wells stayed for the matinee and wrote Sullivan afterward that he had particularly enjoyed a film segment the host had assembled from old Bernhardt and Valentino movies and narrated himself.

In 1936 he began hosting the Harvest Moon Ball for the *Daily News* and included the winners on his vaudeville bill. He toured the country with a show starring Arthur Treacher and Bela Lugosi. The critic in Dayton, Ohio, called it "a fast-moving, highly entertaining show," and described the highlight of the evening: "Bela Lugosi's sepulchral voice is heard offstage with its gruesome haw-haw-haw to the accompaniment of flickering lights, and later he sneaks out behind Treacher who, turning around and facing him, suddenly extends his hand and cracks, 'Dr. Lugosi, I presume!' "

Ed Sullivan entered the ranks of Broadway producers in 1941 when he took over the flop play *Crazy with the Heat*, starring Willie Howard and Luella Gear, and tried to turn it into a hit. After the show closed, he added the dance team of Mary Raye and Naldi, put in new tunes by songwriter Lew Brown, reduced the price scale by 25 percent and reopened it. Brooks Atkinson wrote: "Being a person of unusual compassion, Mr. Sullivan, the celebrated columnist, hated to see all the good things going to waste. . . . Mr. Sullivan improved the second half," but the changes were "not sufficient." After ninety-two performances *Crazy with the Heat* succumbed to prostration.

Sullivan still managed to salvage his salvage job by cutting the second version to an hour and booking it into Loew's State. Business was so good that this became the fifth show in the history of the theater to be held over for a second week.

He had another encounter with the Broadway stage when he produced *Harlem Cavalcade,* an all-Negro show. It was 1942 when Negro performers and musicians were largely unemployed.

His other experience with the legitimate theater was, strangely enough, as a performer. From August 2 to August 7, 1955, Ed Sullivan made his first and final appearance as a stage actor in a summer-stock production of *King of Hearts,* by Jean Kerr and Eleanor Brooks, in Southbury, Connecticut. The role was the minor one of the newspaper publisher, but the reviews were very good. Here is what one critic had to say:

> It is doubtful that any of the millions of television fans who are faithful followers of Ed Sullivan and his CBS "Toast of the Town" ever enjoyed themselves as much as did the sellout crowd which saw Sullivan in his debut as a legitimate actor. It was a gala night at Jack Quinn's Southbury Playhouse. The largest crowd in the history of this little summer theater, which had been equipped with extra seats, rocked with laughter as Sullivan quipped and laughed his way through the part of publisher Joe Wicks.
>
> From his first act appearance through a final informal curtain-call chitchat with the audience, it was evident he loved it—and his watchers did too. Sullivan fitted the role perfectly, showed no signs of stage fright, and had sufficient poise to ad-lib on occasion to send his audience, as well as other members of the cast, into gales of laughter.

He made his nightclub debut in Las Vegas on July 1, 1958, when he presented a variety show for four weeks at the Desert Inn. He hosted a bill starring Carol Burnett, Julia Meade, Rickie Layne, Velvel and magician Richiardi. The engagement was so successful that he returned the following year for another four weeks beginning June 30, 1959, with a new group of performers including Blossom Seeley and Benny Fields in their last public appearance together a few weeks before Fields died. A third nightclub show featured Marilyn Michaels and John Byner but ended abruptly when Sullivan became sick in the middle of the engagement. The Las Vegas shows meant complicated financial deals involving a weekly salary of over $25,000 and the sale of his Connecticut farm.

His early association with Hollywood was without distinction. In 1932 he appeared in *Big Town Czar* which he wrote, according to *The New York Times*, "in his best water-under-the-bridge style . . . extremely first-personal, quite sentimental and edifyingly moralistic." In 1940 he sold an original story, "Ma, He's Making Eyes at Me" to Universal and it was called "limp and foolish . . . bargain basement." While he lived in Hollywood in the late 1930's he sold another story, "There Goes My Heart," to Universal.

In recent years he performed in *Bye Bye Birdie* and *The Singing Nun,* and some observers are convinced he aided their tremendous box-office success. In both films his name followed the other stars and the billing was: "and Ed Sullivan as himself."

It was announced in 1955 that Ed Sullivan was going to go to Hollywood for two months "while he stars in that ultimate tribute to a living celebrity, a Warner Brothers film-biography called 'The Ed Sullivan Story.' " The film was to be made in October of that year with Ed Sullivan as producer and star. "Although the subject matter was not revealed, it is presumed that the film will be autobiographical in nature, with Mr. Sullivan playing himself," according to an early account of the venture. Later it was reported that the project was scrapped after a disagreement between Sullivan and the writer Warner Brothers sent to New York.

In the script, which was supposed to be based on fact, Mrs. Sullivan, chief caretaker of the grandchildren, tells her husband she will divorce him if he does not stop devot-

ing himself to television to the exclusion of everything
else. In reality Mrs. Sullivan has always been delighted by
Ed's involvement with the show; her Catholic husband
would reject divorce even if the marriage hadn't been happy,
and at that time the grandchildren lived in another city.
The plot also used the unlikely situation of Sullivan's
learning about his NBC opposition show fifteen minutes
before air and then changing his own guests for competitive
reasons. A newspaper account described the scrapping of
"The Ed Sullivan Story":

> Mr. Sullivan took a look at the script and told the writer
> it wouldn't do. He asked the writer to go to twenty homes
> and ask people why they watch his program. The writer said
> that wasn't necessary. Mr. Sullivan asked the writer to sit
> down and work out a new script. The writer said he cannot
> write in New York and besides he had left all his pipes back
> in Hollywood. Mr. Sullivan recommended several good pipe
> shops. The writer said he had to have his own pipes. Mr. Sul-
> livan canceled the movie.

During the Second World War the variety shows took a
patriotic turn. "I was too young for World War One and
two old for World War Two so I did the next best thing."

He staged wartime fund-raising rallies and took troupes
to hospitals and camps. He staged a massive show for Army
Emergency Relief and grossed a record $226,500 and sur-
passed that figure a year later with an American Red Cross
Benefit at Madison Square Garden where he grossed $249,-
000. "These were the most fantastic shows that any city
ever has seen. The boxes, each of which I named after a
World War Two hero, sold for five thousand dollars, front-
row seats for a hundred dollars apiece."

In addition he organized the entertainment program at

Halloran General Hospital on Staten Island and brought performers to St. Albans, Kingsbridge, Plattsburg, Cherry Point and other military hospitals.

On one Christmas show at Halloran, Sullivan used Babe Ruth, Benny Leonard and Bruce Cabot as Santa Clauses. At the last minute he phoned Beatrice Lillie, whose son had been killed in the war, and she canceled her own Christmas plans because "I much prefer to spend Christmas with wounded kids."

There is one Halloran show Ed Sullivan remembers before all others. Sullivan was scheduled for a show there and received a phone call from the Halloran chaplain, Father Delaney, who said the soldiers read that Jimmy Durante was in town and wondered if he would join the troupe. Sullivan called Durante at the Astor and discovered he had a bad cold and was also scheduled to do two radio programs on the day of the Halloran show, but to Sullivan's surprise Durante said Yes. The two men worked out a precise schedule for Durante to get back for the radio broadcasts, and this involved catching a particular ferry. It meant that Durante could only do one song, but Sullivan reassured him the men would understand and be delighted he came at all.

When Durante arrived at the island, he was kept hidden in the general's office so the men would be surprised. On that particular evening the first shipload of wounded had come in on the liner *Gripsholm*. Most of them had been American prisoners of war, and the Halloran wounded insisted that the newcomers take the best seats on the divans in rows one and two. When Sullivan introduced Durante, the place went wild. The comic did a routine in which he threw sheet music around and ripped the top off his piano. When he finished, the applause was incredible. As he left the stage, Sullivan started to explain that Durante had to rush back to town for a radio date but the comic came out of the wings, grabbed the mike, and went into another number and then a third. "Thanks to Jimmy this was the greatest night the hospital had ever had. The place was pandemonium."

After Sullivan introduced the next act he went backstage and said to Durante, "Are you out of your mind? You'll never make your ferry." Durante told him to look at the front row of the audience. "When I saw that, Ed, I made up my mind that my radio broadcast wasn't so important, and my cold wasn't so important either." Sullivan put his head through the curtain and saw two young lieutenants in the center divan. They had each lost an arm and were applauding by clapping their two remaining hands together.

7

For Sale, With or Without Ed Sullivan

"T_{HE} early days had more heartaches than I care to recall," Sullivan says about his first months on television. "I didn't have enough money to operate with and the technical side of the show was raw and unpolished. At the end of the first year I figured the show had cost me three hundred and seventy dollars from my own pocket. I had thrown back more than my own salary to get better acts."

The television program stemmed from Sullivan's role as host of the Harvest Moon Ball, the annual amateur dance contest sponsored by his paper, the *Daily News* ("You had to be a bookkeeper, a showman and a manager, and you didn't have time to 'freeze.' "). On his twelfth consecutive year in the job, the show originated from Madison Square Garden. Sullivan introduced a number of celebrities onstage and in the audience. They included Bill Robinson, Lena Horne, Jack Benny, Lucille Ball, Jimmy Stewart, Vivian Blaine, Jack Haley, Risë Stevens, Jinx Falkenburg and Ronald Colman. The climax of the evening came when he called Alan Ladd to the stage and asked the crowd of eighteen thousand to sing "Happy Birthday" to him.

The next day Jack Benny phoned and said, "You should have told me the Garden show was being televised." Sullivan was surprised. Several times during the ball men told him to work more directly to cameras on the mezzanine ledge, but he assumed they were newsreel cameras. Instead it was a remote telecast of CBS.

"Ed Sullivan was on television two years before it was invented," says Bob Hope. The actual date was September 3, 1947.

Worthington Miner, then CBS director of program development, saw the show and was impressed by Sullivan's manner as a host. Miner said, "He seemed relaxed and likable."

"If I had dreamed I was on television, I wouldn't have been so relaxed," Sullivan said later.

Sullivan was one of the first men to see the potential of the television medium, and he was eager to have his own show. He came up with the idea of a sports interview program called "Pros and Cons" with golf professionals giving viewers advice on improving their game. He spoke about it to Marlo Lewis of the Blaine Thompson advertising agency, who was to become Sullivan's first television producer, and Lewis got in touch with CBS. The network was not interested in a golf show but was considering a Sunday-night variety series. Miner had not yet decided on a host but wanted someone who was not a brash "performer" type. He recalled Sullivan's hosting of the Harvest Moon Ball and felt his was "the type of manner we wanted for a Sunday-night audience."

In May, 1948, Lewis brought Miner backstage to New York's Roxy Theatre, where Sullivan was playing a three-week vaudeville engagement with his Dawn Patrol Revue.

"Miner outlined what the network had in mind, said it would be the type of thing I'd done at Madison Square Garden and presently was doing in vaudeville. I signed the contract a week later for a thirteen-week series."

One review of that particular stage show proved to be prophetic and may have influenced Miner at the time: "Newspaper columnists as Broadway stage personalities have long since become a passing vogue, and of these only Ed Sullivan of the New York *Daily News* has managed to survive the field."

On May 21, 1948, CBS officially announced the new program:

> Top-ranking performers in New York nightclubs, hotels and stars of movies, stage and radio are to be participating guests of Ed Sullivan, syndicated newspaper columnist, in a full-hour Sunday revue series titled "You're the Top" and tentatively scheduled to begin on the CBS Television Network June 20, 9:00–10:00 P.M., EDST.

The title "You're the Top" did not survive the first press release. The show premiered as "The Toast of the Town" at nine o'clock on Sunday, June 20, 1948, at the Maxine Elliott Theatre on New York's 39th Street. CBS described the setting as "a roof garden with the Manhattan skyline silhouetted against a starlit sky," but by today's standards it was less picturesque than makeshift.

It took thirty-five people to get the program on the air, including an orchestra of fourteen directed by Ray Bloch and a technical crew of six, and the total budget was $1,350. (Today nearly two hundred people work on the show and sponsors pay $372,000 an hour.)

The guests were the young comedy team of Dean Martin

and Jerry Lewis who split a $200 fee—they were recom-
mended by Ed's daughter Betty; pianist Eugene List, just
out of the Army after playing for The Big Three at Pots-
dam, who received $75; singing New York Fireman John
Kokoman, presented for human interest and to build a
local audience, ($25); ballerina Kathryn Lee of *Allegro*
($50); singer Monica Lewis ($50); the six original June
Taylor girls who were called "The Toastettes" ($20 each);
fight referee Ruby Goldstein ($75); the comedy team of
Lee Goodman and Jim Kirkwood, and Richard Rodgers and
Oscar Hammerstein II.

In their segment Rodgers and Hammerstein explained
the music of *South Pacific* and *Oklahoma,* and Rodgers said
that his favorite song was "The Surrey with the Fringe on
Top." Off camera they remarked that they were going to
buy CBS stock with what was left over in the talent budget
for them. Monica Lewis sang a popular tune and forgot
that a microphone was hidden in her bouquet. She threw
out her arms in an eloquent gesture and sent the mike
spinning across the stage. Ruby Goldstein, who refereed
heavyweight championship bouts, was a topical guest and
Sullivan remembers the setting. "We had a corner of a ring
set up on the stage, then Ruby leaned against the ropes and
talked about the big fight coming up between Joe Louis
and Jersey Joe Walcott. It was the first trick set we ever
used."

"When the first show went on the air, I can't say I
thought very much of it," says Ray Bloch, who still directs
the orchestra today.

"I wasn't sure we would last for a second week. I was
a nervous wreck," Sullivan says.

In the press he expressed optimism, "The sky is the limit

in this new field. There are no limits to what can happen
because there are no limits to the eye and ear." He gave this
appraisal of the medium in a magazine article a few months
after he was on the air. Privately there seemed to be no
limit to the financial and technical hardships. "We didn't
have enough money to do many of the things we wanted
to do, and as for the mechanical side, television in 1948
had a most unhappy penchant for slicing off the tops of
heads. I've often been kidded because I don't smile, and you
can imagine what an unsmiling Ed Sullivan looked like with
only half a head."

The biggest handicap of all was the hostile reception
from the television reviewers. Emerson Radio became his
first sponsor when he was on the air a few months, and then
canceled after thirteen weeks. Sullivan was certain that the
main reason was the harsh remarks directed at him in the
press.

"Some of the criticism used to tear my guts out. Here I
was working for nothing, trying to get somewhere. In 1949
networks and advertising agencies knew little about the
medium and so could be influenced easily by writers in
important papers. Small wonder that I couldn't smile into
the TV camera."

The most antagonistic critic was John Crosby, television
reviewer for the influential *Herald Tribune*. When Sullivan
first came on the air, Crosby devoted his entire column to
the program. The headline was "Why? Why? Why?" The
column:

> One of the small but vexing questions confronting anyone
> in this area with a television set is Why is Ed Sullivan on
> it every Sunday night? If the set owner has been properly
> conditioned by soap opera he's likely to add Why? Why?

Why? It's in all respects a darn hard question, almost a jackpot question, and it seems to baffle Mr. Sullivan as much as anyone else. . . . Mr. Sullivan is a persuasive fellow [being able to get performers for so little money, but] . . . if he has any other qualifications for the job, they are not visible on my small screen. . . . It could be a wonderful Sunday night program, and sometimes it is, but what is Ed Sullivan doing there?

Sullivan hit back at Crosby:

Public opinion, I'm certain, would agree that I've contributed more to television in its embryonic state than you have contributed with your reckless and uninformed back-seat driving. You belt away at performers and producers as a means of earning a weekly salary. At least I give them a gracious introduction and a showmanly presentation that enhances their earning power. Your column acquires a tremendous importance. When it is employed to recommend that a man be thrown out of his job it becomes quite an evil instrument.

Jack Gould of *The New York Times* was equally harsh. On July 4, 1948, he wrote a review comparing the host unfavorably with Milton Berle whose program was on NBC.

For a variety revue, where a dominant personality is so helpful in tying up the loose ends, the choice of Ed Sullivan as master of ceremonies seems ill-advised. Since he is a newspaper man there is no reason to expect him to be an actor, but his extreme matter-of-factness, plus his predilection for introducing his friends in the audience, does not add up to very sparkling entertainment. In such a key spot an experienced and versatile person must be in charge if the whole show is to acquire a distinctiveness and fluidity of its own. . . .

CBS has all necessary ingredients for a successful program of variety. Once it appreciates more fully the need for knowing hands to guide the proceedings—both on stage and off—it, too, should have an enjoyable hit.

Sullivan responded with a blistering note. "Jack Gould called up blazing about a letter I wrote and I asked him, 'What are you so hot about? I just put my opinion of you in a personal letter. You spread your opinion of me all over the Sunday *Times*'."

Apparently Gould thought he had a point, because the following Sunday a letter from the host was printed in the "Letters to the Editor" column of the entertainment section:

> You object to "Ed Sullivan's predilection for introducing his friends in the audience," on the grounds that it "slows up the show." If the introductions were of nondescript characters, or of my grocer or butcher, you'd be on firm ground, but when the introductions bring to the television camera the retired undefeated heavyweight champion, Joe Louis; the manager of the Brooklyn Dodgers, Leo Durocher; Tin Pan Alley's Richard Rodgers, I seriously question that your reaction is shared by the video audience. . . .
>
> As to your opinion of me as master of ceremonies, I won't challenge that because difference of opinion makes horse racing. However, I do feel that when you compare me with a Milton Berle, you misunderstand my position on our show. They wanted a working newspaperman, sufficiently versed in show business, to nominate acts that could live up to a "Toast of the Town" designation. As it is a Sunday show, they wanted a certain measure of dignity and restraint, rather than a vain attempt to work with acrobats, tumblers, etc., which Berle does brilliantly.

At this time Betty Sullivan was sixteen and the attacks against her father became so rough that she stopped reading the reviews. Sylvia Sullivan remembers when Emerson Radio canceled. "I'll never forget that day we received notification that our first sponsor, Emerson, wasn't renewing. The program had been on only six months. I was the first to hear the cancellation news and I want to tell you I was absolutely sunk. I was home all alone that day when the phone rang. You can't imagine how sick I was. That evening we were out having dinner, and some of the fans came over to compliment the program. We both felt so empty we just sat there with sinking hearts."

Soon afterward came an episode that upset Ed Sullivan even more. He was shocked and infuriated to learn that CBS was trying to sell "The Toast of the Town" to prospective advertisers "with or without Ed Sullivan." The sales department felt sponsors were being scared away by the criticism of Sullivan in the press.

"At first I couldn't believe what had happened. I've never been so hurt or angry before or since. That was my low point on television and maybe the low point of my life."

Sullivan made his feelings known in loud, angry tones that resounded through the CBS executive offices. "I got out of radio before it was really big, and I was determined not to make the same mistake on television." He was given an apology and told that the optional offer had originated with a single executive, Jack Van Volkenburg, and had not been approved by the company. Bill Paley and Frank Stanton, the two chief officers of CBS, let him know they had been unaware of Van Volkenburg's action and did not support it in any way. Van Volkenburg has since died, but even now Sullivan cannot forgive him.

It was Mercury's General Sales Manager Joe Bayne who came to the host's rescue and grabbed the show for the Ford Motor Company. Bayne, who had once worked with Major Bowes of "The Amateur Hour," said, "It took us less than twenty minutes to decide on Ed Sullivan. It was crystal clear Ed was a second Major Bowes. Bowes used to muff the English language. Ed does too. But the thing about the two of them is their genuineness and truthfulness, so we said we'll buy Sullivan for thirteen weeks." The thirteen weeks lengthened into an association of many years and ended forever the problem of finding a sponsor for the program.

But the venom of many critics never abated. After four years John Crosby wrote:

"I regret," said Ed Sullivan on one of his shows, "that I'm handicapped by no talent at all." That's carrying candor to almost embarrassing lengths, but it states the case rather accurately. Last Sunday, though, Sullivan had us all pretty worried. He got mixed up in a talking-horse act. While this isn't exactly a wild-animal act, it is definitely a tame-animal act which requires a certain amount of talent. For a moment I thought he'd get thrown out of the lodge but, no, he displayed absolutely no talent at all in handling this talking horse which showed a disposition not to tell him a damn thing, not even whether he planned to run for President. Mr. Sullivan's amateur standing remains pristine but it was a close thing.

After eight years Crosby wrote: "Mr. Sullivan, of course, is notoriously and admittedly without talent."

In time, Jack Gould revised his evaluation and wrote on the eighteenth anniversary: "He is unquestionably one of the medium's great intuitive showmen."

One thing time has not altered is Sullivan's sensitivity to criticism.

"I hate adverse criticism. I loathe it. I will never get used to it. Furthermore I suspect anybody who says he is immune to it is being a really big liar. You get a very possessive feeling about each show and each act. Actually they are all your beloved. You don't get hardened to criticism. When they kicked me around as a performer that was justifiable, but nobody can tell me how to routine a vaudeville show. As for acts, I'm familiar with more show-business acts than anybody around. The original panning I got bit into me very deeply. Sure I've been hurt by the jokes about my act. I'm accustomed to them now but they hurt. What I really want, I guess, is for people to tell me I look like Robert Goulet." What form of dissent does he find most jarring? "All of it."

The host has never kept his opinions of a review to himself. "Probably some of the most scathing and long letters ever received by television critics have come from Mr. Sullivan," said one of the critics, Val Adams of *The New York Times.*

Some short ones too. To Harriet Van Horne, who said that "He got where he is not by having a personality but by having no personality; he is the commonest common denominator." Sullivan wrote: "Dear Miss Van Horne, You bitch. Sincerely, Ed Sullivan."

Atra Baer, longtime family friend who was an entertainment writer for the *Journal-American,* once criticized a Sullivan show. His response was 50 percent longer than to Harriet Van Horne. "Dear Miss Baer, *Et tu,* Atra? Sincerely, Ed Sullivan."

Recently Sullivan described the letter-writing ritual of the past. "I used to sit down in the evening and write a letter. Sylvia would come in and say 'type it up, put it in an envelope, seal it, put a stamp on it and then, when you're all done, tear it up.' I would do everything except tear it up, and then, when she went inside, I would slip out of the room, run out to the mailbox and mail it. She would come

back and ask me what I had done with the letter and I would
say that I had torn it up."

Sullivan has mellowed a little, but he can still be out-
spoken in expressing his views. He was justifiably proud
of a program from Expo 67 and dismayed by what he
felt was unjust criticism from a New York television
writer. "He called me on the telephone and chewed me
out for fifteen minutes," the newspaperman said.

To a large extent the years have taught him to accept
the ribbing he gets without being resentful. He has even
learned to laugh at the remarks about him, even though
he has inspired some of the deadliest one liners in America.

Best known are Fred Allen's "Ed Sullivan will be a success as long as other people have talent" and Joe E. Lewis'
"Ed Sullivan is the only man who can brighten up a room
by leaving it."

Carl Reiner said: "Love is like Ed Sullivan. You can't
explain its hold on you, but after a while you take it for
granted."

The *World-Telegram* said in 1958, "He wasn't well enough
known to sit down in the audience so they used him on the
show."

A motion-picture critic wrote in a review of *The Singing
Nun:* "What can you say about a film in which the best
performance is given by Ed Sullivan?"

Kate Cameron's review of the same film said: "Ed plays
himself on the screen and does a very good job of it. He
seems as much at ease before the Metro color cameras as
he is before the CBS TV lens." She probably intended to
be serious.

Judith Crist left no doubt about her intentions: "The
events and 'characters' we are told are fictitious, including,

we suppose, Ed Sullivan who portrays 'himself.' " She is more direct later in the same column: "Ed Sullivan plays Ed Sullivan grimly."

Jack Benny: "What would happen, Ed, if you weren't here to introduce the acts? As a friend, let me give you some advice. Don't ever stay home to find out." When Benny announced Sullivan would be a guest on his forthcoming television special, he said, "He'll be dynamic. He's going to walk and everything."

Hal Humphrey: "The Forest Lawn Cemetery is trying to buy commercials on the show."

Joey Bishop was called upon to speak at an Ed Sullivan dinner: "I have been asked to talk about the generosity, warmth and honesty of Ed Sullivan. Thank you." Exit Bishop.

Henry Youngman: "In Africa the cannibals adored him. They thought he was some new kind of frozen food."

Earl Wilson: "Ed Sullivan knows what the public likes and one of these days he's going to give it to them."

George Jessel: "Ed is a great man. He belongs on Mount Rushmore with Washington and Jefferson and Lincoln. In fact you don't have to chisel him out of stone. He's ready right now."

Soupy Sales: "The real reason the circus comes to town is to see Ed Sullivan."

Bing Crosby: "While he doesn't sing, dance or tell jokes, he does them equally well."

Bob Hope: "I always figured The Ed Sullivan Theater would be a wax museum."

Jack Carter: "I'd mail you a present, but what do you give a man who has nothing?" Other Carterisms: "When Ed got off the plane at Anchorage, the Eskimos screamed

and ran away. They thought a totem pole had landed."
"Was the ground cold when you came up this morning?"
"The amount of talent you have will never wear out."
"Don't cross your arms or they may bury you."
Joe E. Lewis: "Ed has personality but not for a human
being." He also said, "He was a greeter at Forest Lawn
Cemetery on the coast but quit in self-defense when they
tried to bury him on three different occasions."
Fred Allen: "What does Sullivan do? He points at people.
Rub meat on actors and dogs will do the same." This time
Sullivan had an answer: "Maybe Fred should rub some
meat on a sponsor."
Occasionally the remark is even nice as well as funny.
Alan King: "Ed does nothing, but he does it better than
anyone else on television."
The distinctive manner and appearance have made him
a ripe target for mimicry and the most satirized man in
America. LBJ and Bobby Kennedy, other leading candi-
dates for the title, arrived late on the national scene and
will probably leave it long before Sullivan has presented
his final program.
"I never realized that I looked that way and talked that
way until people started mimicking me. One of them has
a round face himself, but when he goes into the imitation
he looks just like me, he sounds just like me, and it frac-
tures me."
At first the imitators used to hurt and irritate him but
he was not only laughing himself but booking them by
1953. In March of that year he presented Will Jordan,
first of the mimics (the list later included Sammy Davis,
Jack Carter, Jack E. Leonard, John Byner and Johnny
Carson). He saw Jordan after his friend Joe Moore told

him to watch the comic on a local television program. Sullivan tuned in and roared with laughter. He called the studio on the phone to speak to Jordan. "Hello, this is Ed Sullivan," he said, and Jordan replied, "That's nice. This is Marlene Dietrich." The comic insisted on calling Sullivan back at home and was very embarrassed when he realized he was talking to the genuine article.

"Will Jordan exaggerates my mannerisms until he is more like me than I am myself. He used to sit glued in front of the television set every Sunday night until he could mimic me. People like that have a special oral faculty. When he does me he changes his voice until it's right on the button. I can close my eyes, stand off in the wings and tell myself I am hearing my own voice." And, in fact, Jordan *was* Ed Sullivan's voice in the Broadway stage production of *Bye Bye Birdie.*

When Sullivan is the target, the wit is often acid rather than friendly. The Cardiff Giant, the Cigar-Store Indian, a stone-faced monument just off the boat from Easter Island, Smiley, the Great Stone Face, Poker Face, the Walking Wooden Indian, the Toast of the Tomb, Mr. Rigor Mortis, the Sleepwalker, the Miltown Maestro, an artistic basket case and Rock of Ages are a few of the phrases that have been used to describe him.

"He moves like a sleepwalker; his smile is that of a man sucking a lemon; his speech is frequently lost in a thicket of syntax; his eyes pop from their sockets or sink so deep in their bags that they seem to be peering up at the camera from the bottom of twin wells." This is how *Time* magazine saw him in their cover story.

"Stony-faced, baggy-eyed, so stiff through his bull neck and shoulders that he is frequently assumed to have broken his back, a mangler of thought and language, a stumbling, bungling, fumbling perpetual amateur who has yet to master the smallest gesture, the simplest phrase, Sullivan is the most painfully unlikely stage figure in all of the bizarre history of vaudeville." This was *Newsweek*.

"As he ushers acts on and off, Sullivan's hands still hover helplessly about the region of his tie and nose, and his eyes still shift restlessly toward some distant field beyond camera range, suggesting something halfway between hope and fear that the theater is on fire and he will be liberated before the hour is over." So said Helen Dudar in a New York *Post* profile.

"There is no doubt that by conventional standards Sullivan is the worst master of ceremonies who ever was on land or sea. He starts involved sentences he can't really finish; he summons guests from the audience to the stage and then doesn't know what to do with them once they're there; and he will, when there's time to fill toward the end, persist in asking those out front the most embarrassing of all questions: 'Well, how did you like our show tonight? Did you have a good time?' (Applause)." This is Phil Minoff in *Cue* magazine.

Sullivan's description of himself is no more flattering: "I have a very thick neck for a man my size. It is size seventeen and it is out of proportion to the rest of me.... I have a big neck because of the way the upper part of my body is built and it's that construction that makes me walk the way I do.... The high cheekbones and deep-set eyes give me a naturally lugubrious look and on top of that I am basically shy. So I'm not an easy laugher unless I'm talking to somebody onstage. It's almost impossible for me to laugh into the metal and exterior of a camera."

This self-critical, self-defending showman is the only person to perform a superhuman feat of endurance and last for two decades on television. His survival has baffled the experts and given rise to a second pastime besides criticizing: explaining. There have been at least thirty explanations for Ed Sullivan's success:

1. Showmanship. "He's the greatest showman since Barnum."—Johnny Wayne.

2. Naturalness. "Many TV people boast, give me two weeks with that show and I'd really make it into something good. They want to slick it up. If they did, it would be two years on the air. Ed can run forever."—Frank Shuster.

3. Hard work. "Sullivan works harder than anyone else in the business."—Nat Hiken.

4. Routining. "Routining—pacing and contrasting acts—is Ed's tremendous knack."—Bob Precht.

5. Spontaneity. "What really makes our program a success is its surprise element. The only thing certain about the Sullivan show is that the first act opens it."—Mark Leddy.

6. Sincerity. "For most people he is an endearing figure, embodying in his consummate ineptitude all the sincerity, straightforwardness, and democratic virtue that slicker articles lack."—*Newsweek*.

7. His presence. "There's no secret. The key is Ed's distinctive, strong personality. He has enormous acceptance around the country."—Bob Precht.

8. His absence. "He tells the facts and then gets out of the way."—Dave Garroway.

9. Universal appeal. "There's something for everybody, of every age and every taste."—Margaret MacManus.

10. Lack of appeal. "Ed has never lost his appeal because he did not have any to start with."—Pat Weaver. (It was 1955 and Weaver was president of NBC television. He went on: "This season we've got Martin and Lewis. He can be taken.")

11. Topicality. "His news instinct is among the sharpest in show business."—*Look*.

12. Squareness. "While everyone else is trying to be 'hip,' Sullivan is satisfied to be a square."—The Oakland *Tribune*.

13. Brevity. "Editing down a lot of acts really improves them."—Bob Precht.

14. Lack of brevity. "Each of the attractions has had plenty of room in which to operate."—*Cue's* Phil Minoff.

15. Good taste. "One reason for Ed's success is his inherent good taste."—Leland Hayward.

16. Mediocrity. "Sullivan has a wonderful sense of the mediocre."—Russell Lynes.

17. Ruthlessness. "Ed Sullivan retains his own unseen gifts—shrewd scrambling ambition to reach the satisfaction of success. . . . He wars constantly with anyone or anything he suspects might impede his success."—Jack O'Brian.

18. Compassion. "Ed Sullivan *lives* democracy. He has a big heart and a king-size compassion for his fellow beings. It is that dimension of his Sunday-night show that attracts and holds his audience of multimillions."—Ralph Bunche.

19. Booking talent. "He's a genius at picking talent." —Alexander Cohen.

20. Lack of talent. "It isn't necessary to know how to dance, sing or tell jokes to be a success on TV. The fact is, if Sullivan had been able to do any of those things, his TV career would have ended years ago."—Hal Humphrey.

21. Daring. "He has a newspaperman's daring."—Jack O'Brian.

22. Undaring. "He's here to stay because he does a nice simple job of running his show. Hit-you-over-the-head performers aren't going to wind up making the money in television. It's like Daniel Boone. He pioneered through the woods but he didn't make the money. It took the lumber companies to do that."—Fred Allen.

23. A feeling for performers. "Appreciation is one of the rarest, most wondrous of God's gifts when it's real, and Ed's is. He is so aware of talent, so struck with the splendors of it

—so altogether stagestruck in the true sense of the phrase—
that one can actually *feel* it."—Helen Hayes.

24. A feeling for the audience. "He has a natural feeling
for the mental level of his audience which is subterranean."
—Fred Allen.

25. Uniqueness. "He has invented a whole new form of
television. It's entirely his own which explains why copyists
have failed."—Leland Hayward.

26. Averageness. "People seem to identify themselves with
him, possibly because he is so unassuming and because he
often appears as ill at ease as a quiet family man recruited
by his wife to be the reluctant m.c. of a parent-teachers' entertainment."—Richard Gehman.

27. Involvement. "He's totally involved. He is out every
night—at the theater or catching acts at nightclubs—always
on the hunt for talent. He has more energy than most
younger men in this business."—Bob Precht.

28. The X factor. "He has a basically likable quality that
viewers respond to—a quality X, unknown and beyond logical analysis."—Don Freeman.

29. Intuitiveness. "He's a guy whose show-business judgment is just about infallible. He seems to know untuitively
what other impresarios have to learn by surveys."—*Cue*'s
Phil Minoff.

30. Quality. "The answer is that Ed puts on a very
good vaudeville show every week."—Steve Allen (his former competitor).

Sullivan himself explains his survival in sixteen different
ways, depending on his mood:

1. "You can't get away from one thing and that's the
hard work that has gone into the show over the years. That
I think is the reason why we've lasted so long."

2. "What has saved me and the show is something apparently I was born with: the ability to pick acts and material
for acts that a national audience will enjoy. It's an instinct
you have or haven't got."

3. "The fellow who says, 'The heck with it, nobody is going to stop me,' is the one who gets ahead. That's the way I felt when I was twenty-one. Nothing could stop me. I've never stopped being grateful that I had that attitude. It was the most important single factor that helped me get ahead and I'm hanging on to it."

4. "Frankly I think our show has lasted because from the first show my craggy features aroused the protective instincts of the country. Probably people said to themselves, 'This poor fellow looks so miserably unhappy we've got to help him out.' "

5. "If you respect your audience, it respects you. People know darn well that we respect them. That's why we're still around."

6. "There's one reason for our success. Every other variety show has always had a star as performer. I don't think you can ever get anybody but me content to just introduce an act and get off. The most difficult thing in the world is to shut up."

7. "My experience as a newspaperman is the reason why we've lasted. I approach the show and put it together the way a reporter handles a story. Because of my background I developed an instinct and a sensitivity to public trends. For the same reason that every newspaper in the country ran the firing of La Rosa on page one, I grabbed him for the show. I knew it was the hottest TV news in years." (Sullivan remembers wryly that in 1948 Milton Berle told him: "Now, Ed, you're a newspaperman. You leave show business to me.")

8. "I am sincerely rooting for each act to click. The more applause an act gets the happier I am."

9. "On TV I've been myself and it's the only thing that saved me. If I'd tried to whip up a phony smile, if I'd tried to be an actor or tell stories, the public would have tossed me the hell out."

10. "After all I'm a routiner. It's my specialty. We edit very carefully after dress rehearsal. We never give them too

much of anything. It's the best vaudeville, literally, and it's fast-paced."

11. "We've never believed in a stock company but in different acts every week."

12. "A taped program lacks a certain earthliness.... A light will go out. Something will be said wrong. That's okay. I'd rather have something go wrong and let the people know that the show was live than correct and polish the tape."

13. "I think my awkwardness on camera is the real reason I am still here today. It has aroused the mother instinct of America."

14. "The secret of my success is that I'm an average American and the show reflects my taste."

15. "The basis of our show and the reason for its popularity is public acceptance. We have a family show with something for everyone. It's healthy entertainment."

16. "I think people identify with me. I'm not a performer. I'm a host. Sort of like some ordinary guy from Iowa who somehow met someone famous and is throwing a party for his friends and says, 'Hey, look who I got!' "

Of course there is no single answer. During his early years a critic suggested that the reason for Sullivan's success was that stars came on his show because he was a powerful and influential columnist. His logical reply: "If that's all there is to putting on a show, let the opposition hire itself another columnist." If there were a simple formula for longevity, the other networks would have followed it. Even so, people continue searching for the correct explanation, and that includes Sullivan himself. "What have I got?" he once asked a friend. The response: "I don't know, but you've got it."

8

How Am I Going to
Explain It to the Lion?

"I DON'T make any stars. I simply give people the opportunity to prove themselves. They have to have it in them in the first place. If they don't, a million of my shows wouldn't do them any good."

Sullivan does not believe that anyone can "make a star." What he can do, and does with unequaled skill, is recognize talent. Richard Gehman says: "He has a kind of radar set built into his personality which enables him to spot the fresh, the intriguing and the potentially popular."

Sullivan gets many of the acts himself and finds them in a variety of places—even auctions. One spring when he was in London, he and Laurence Harvey made a successful bid for the joint purchase of the Balaklava Bugle which had sounded the charge that sent the Light Brigade thundering into "The Valley of Death" in the Crimea. In a television segment he gave the bugle back to the 17/21 Lancers, the regiment to which "The 600" belonged.

What guides him in putting together his show is "what

I believe the public will like the most. It must be entertaining. That is the ultimate consideration." He is strongly influenced by acts which have been successful somewhere else first—nightclubs, records, circuses.

Helping him in his search is a network of informal talent scouts. He hears about new acts from guests on the show and from talent agents who will go to Ed Sullivan first because he pays well, he can boost a performer's career, and he will be around to reciprocate favors after other hosts have left the air.

A friend of Mrs. Sullivan recommended an unknown instrumental group called the Tijuana Brass, and CBS Board Chairman William Paley tipped Sullivan onto an obscure comic named Dick Van Dyke.

Sometimes the bookings will come from the public at large. "People send us postcards about acts from all over Europe, from such obscure places that you have to get a map to track them down. Elevator operators and cab drivers will give you tips. One cab driver told me about a magician he had seen when he was stationed in Munich and we got him and he was fine."

On another occasion a stranger sitting next to Mrs. Sullivan under a hair dryer at the beauty parlor told her about two youngsters in Jamaica. "We flew a scout down there, and they were just as good as the lady had said."

His daughter Betty told him about Rosemary Clooney and Martin and Lewis, Nat "King" Cole told him about Rickie Layne and Velvel, Mimi Benzell helped him to book Margaret Truman, and he heard about an act called the Australian Woodchoppers from a man who used to cover vaudeville in Chicago named Carl Sandburg.

Sullivan suspects that his is the only program on tele-

vision that ever had Governor Herman Talmadge of Georgia
as a talent scout. The Governor, who was noted for his
segregationist views, was responsible for the booking of a
Negro. "Some years back Governor Talmadge sent me a
letter and said, 'Ed, we have a wonderful performer down
here. He can cover up the piano with a big heavy cloth on
it, and he can play as you never heard anybody play.' So
I made the arrangements with Governor Talmadge and up
came his protégé who was just as great as he said."

Ballerina Nanci Crompton telephoned Sullivan from Buf-
falo to tell him about a performer appearing at a nightclub
up there. "She said he was creating a riot among the teen-
agers with his singing, and she asked me to come see him.
I heard him and thought he was quite terrific."

Sullivan made arrangements for an appearance with the
singer's agent, who was surprised that the host knew about
his client. The singer was unknown when he was signed,
but by the date of the performance his records of "The
Little White Cloud That Cried" and "Cry" had made
Johnny Ray a star.

Sullivan operates well under pressure and has an uncanny ability for spotting popular acts just when the competition is keenest. In 1958 he booked comedy in the first
half of his show to meet the competition of "Maverick."
When Steve Allen challenged him in the ratings, he countered with Elvis Presley. When Walt Disney cut into his
audience, he brought over the Beatles, the Dave Clark Five
and other English groups. "My competition has been trying to knock me off for years. I wish they'd stop trying.
The ideal setup is where you have nothing at all against
you. I'm working for that."

The graveyard of old programs he has laid to rest includes "Philco Playhouse," "Supper Club," "The Big Pay-off," "The Amateur Hour," "Bowling Stars," "Scott Island," "Suspicion," "Anybody Can Play," "Dragnet," "Pete Kelly's Blues," "Music on Ice," "The Tab Hunter Show," "National Velvet," "Car 54, Where Are You?," "Sir Francis Drake," "Follow the Sun," "Grindl," "Jamie McPheeters," "Arrest and Trial," "Empire," "The Bill Dana Show," "Broadside," "Branded," "Buckskin" and "Hey, Landlord." His toughest competitors were "The Colgate Comedy Hour," "Maverick," "Lawman," "The Steve Allen Show" and "Wagon Train."

The opposition for his first show on June 20, 1948 (broadcast on six stations as opposed to 196 today), included two feature films, *Gentleman from Dixie* with Jack LaRue and Marion Marsh and *Jimmy Steps Out* with Jimmy Stewart and Paulette Goddard. Senator Robert Taft was on NBC in a convention interview program from Philadelphia.

In later years the competition was more difficult. NBC threw Perry Como into the opposing Sunday-night spot during the 1949–50 season and after that tried head-liners like Bob Hope, Martin and Lewis, Jimmy Durante and Eddie Cantor. The network's notable programming failure almost inspired a television play. It was reported in the late 1950's that NBC commissioned Paddy Chayefsky to prepare a sixty-minute drama entitled "The Man Who Knocked Off Ed Sullivan," but the project was quietly abandoned.

The flexibility of Sullivan's format and his ingenuity as a showman have been difficult obstacles for the opposition to overcome. "You've got to keep growing and experimenting—that is, if you want to stay in a young and growing form of entertainment like television." He said this in 1952 and reiterates the words today.

In 1952 "The Colgate Comedy Hour" was providing tough competition. "Television was becoming fairly well cluttered with variety shows and there was a sameness about 'Toast' which wasn't healthy. When my vacation rolled around, I decided to spend as much time as necessary to do something about a face-lifting for the show. Then one night I was doing a piece on Oscar Hammerstein for my column, and the thought struck me that television biographies of top show people could be fascinating." He telephoned Hammerstein, who became his first subject, and a new television trend was established.

The efforts of "The Colgate Comedy Hour" to beat Sullivan on March 21, 1955, were the subject of a *Life* magazine story. On that Sunday NBC assembled Gordon MacRae and four Gabors in New York on the gangway of a superliner, the S.S. *United States*. Sullivan's guests included Lillian Roth, dancers Mata and Hari, the All-American basketball team, Alfred G. Vanderbilt and Joe Jackson, Jr. *Life* wrote: "Audience surveys showed that the superliner with its Gabors could not top the 'Toast' talent. Next move a fleet of supercarriers?"

In booking talent, as in everything else, Sullivan acts quickly and instinctively. The newsman in him is accustomed to running an exclusive story immediately before another reporter gets it. Unless he is intentionally waiting until an act is at the crest of its popularity (such as a singer with a new record) he does not postpone presenting a new discovery.

At a charity luncheon at the Statler Hilton Hotel he saw a novelty act called the Jovers. In the middle of their routine he stood up, spoke into the microphone and said, "I want to get that act." They were on before the month was out.

In 1967 he auditioned a nine-year-old girl named Tania Solnik at a Sunday dress rehearsal and signed her for that evening. She opened the program and was a tremendous success.

On the day of his 1960 St. Patrick's Day Show a Canadian singer named Denyse Ange dropped by the studio to meet him at Wayne and Shuster's suggestion. Sullivan said Hello, chatted briefly and asked her if she knew any Irish songs. She said Yes—"When Irish Eyes Are Smiling"—and on the spur of the moment he signed up the startled singer for the show a few hours later.

Shani Wallis, an English singer and actress who played the title role in *Irma La Douce* on the London stage, made her American television debut on the Sullivan show on April 8, 1962, on two hours' notice. Sullivan decided at 6 P.M. on Sunday that there was a gap on the program which Shani Wallis could fill beautifully. He had seen her perform earlier in the week at the Persian Room of the Plaza Hotel.

Once Sullivan decided at the last minute that an eight-minute dancing act was dull and told a booking agent at the theater to "get me that girl fiddler we were discussing yesterday." The man rushed to the telephone and called the girl who happened to be spending Sunday evening at home. She got dressed, grabbed her violin, leaped into a taxi and reached the CBS studio in time for the final few minutes of the show.

The impulsiveness sometimes brings regrets. He can

agree to more money than necessary or sign an untried newcomer for several appearances when one with options would
do. He went to the Upstairs at the Downstairs nightclub on
a Thursday night and on the spot booked the performers for two appearances, the first for that coming Sunday.
Their number was not successful, so he paid them off and
told them he'd look at them again when they had more
experience.

Sometimes the spontaneous booking is an act of charity.
Sullivan has given bookings instead of straight handouts to
many once-famous actors who were down-and-out. That
way he contributed to a performer's self-respect as well as
his finances.

Signing acts is not always a quick and easy matter, and
the top shows sometimes compete vigorously for headliners.
Agents know that Sullivan is a fair man to negotiate with
but the wrong person to double-cross.

Marcel Marceau knows this better than anyone. When
Marceau opened in New York with a one-man show, Sullivan went backstage and spoke to the Frenchman and his
manager about a Sullivan show appearance. The manager
told Sullivan that he had been talking to Max Lieb-
man about a television appearance. Sullivan appreciated
the honesty and said that his offer to Marceau still stood.

Later the manager telephoned Sullivan to say that Marceau had signed for a spectacular on Sunday opposite the
Sullivan show. Sullivan still did not object and said he
would take Marceau for two shows provided he made no
other television appearances. The manager agreed and they
settled on a $5,000 fee.

Later the manager informed Sullivan that Marceau had

to have sole control of the lighting, camera work and the orchestra. Sullivan explained, as he always does in such cases, that he insists on the final say on his own program, but that he is eager to show off performers to the best advantage. He said there would be no problem in satisfying the Frenchman and having him pleased with the presentation. "I told him I'd talk it over with Marceau at rehearsal." The manager agreed and the deal was still on. Then Sullivan read in the newspapers that Marceau had signed for a Chevrolet program. Sullivan's contract was not in writing but he still considered it binding. He phoned the manager and made his feelings clear. The manager disagreed.

A week or so later Sullivan went to the Baronet Theatre in New York where, along with the feature film, he saw a short subject of Marceau doing four of his specialties. Sullivan checked and found he could buy the television rights in the United States without the permission of Marceau or his manager, but the contract stipulated that the Marceau four-part short could not be broken up into segments but had to run in full. Sullivan was going to Paris on business and decided to meet with the people who owned the television rights while he was there. By paying an extra $2,500, he obtained a new clause in the contract enabling him to show the routines on four different Sundays. "It was a case of cheating cheaters," Sullivan says today, recalling the episode.

There is no aspect of Sullivan's relationship with performers that causes more comment in the trade than his penchant for editing.

Jack Carter says, "Of course, the big bit on Sullivan's show is timing. You're booked to do twelve minutes. In rehearsal it's cut to eight, in dress to four. Then Ed calls you

before air and asks, 'Could you stay in your hotel and phone
it in?' "

Says Sullivan, "No performer thinks he gets enough time.
However, we have worked the program to a formula and
believe we know how much viewers will take. We get together with a performer and his agent and go over the act.
We'll cut out a segment from a comedy act and the comedian's agent will say, 'but we've got our best laughs with
that.' And we say, 'well, we don't think it fits onto our
show.' "

His feelings today are the same as in 1948 when he wrote:
"Brevity is the soul of wit on television." He feels that the
main reason performers misunderstand the editing is the
difference between nightclubs and television. "A comedian
who works in a nightclub has perhaps forty minutes to do
his act. His audience is there for the evening. TV audiences
have to be won quickly. Home viewers can switch to other
channels."

He finds the roughest part of his job is dealing with a
comic and a manager after cuts have been made. "Some of
them must think they're talking to a lunatic when their
routine is slashed. They always look as if I've slapped them
in the face, but I'm usually right."

It bothers him but he's learned to do what's best for the
show, although occasionally humanity overrules programming. "A blind guitarist did a number which just didn't
work at dress rehearsal and he was taken off that night's
show. Later his wife made a touching plea for another
chance and, with his act edited to its strong points, he was
a great hit."

Editing has produced many strange stories. The Frediannis are still bewildered by memories of the evening they presented their bicycle act on the show. Their routine involved three tricks, but after dress rehearsal they were told to do just the last two. They were scheduled for the end of the program but it ran long and they were informed in the middle of the hour that they would only be able to do the second half of their climactic trick. When they finally came on camera, it was so late that they were only seen climbing onto their bicycles and that was under the filmed credits.

On another occasion a clown act was cut in half after dress rehearsal. Somehow everybody was informed except orchestra leader Ray Bloch, who naturally went into the opening bars of the deleted portion. Sullivan took the fastest method of correcting the error and while the clown was performing he said to Bloch and a nationwide audience: "This number has been cut in half, so start the music later, Ray."

Another episode could have been dangerous and was complicated by the language barrier. A Spanish aerialist on the show had so much equipment that his act had to be taped in the afternoon for presentation that evening. The man had been told that his routine was being cut, but with his limited knowledge of English he did not understand. He was sitting in the audience watching the show, and when he saw the abbreviated tape of his act he became hysterical and tried to rush onstage. As the usher restrained him, he was saying in his native tongue, as a translator later explained, "I want to tell the people of America that's not my act." When the show went off the air, Sullivan met with the man against the advice of police who had been called to the theater and feared he was violent. Sullivan handled the situation with great aplomb and promised the aerialist three minutes on his show the following week. The man refused to believe it "because Ed Sullivan's word does not mean anything anymore." Seven days later he found out differently.

Some of the changes made after dress rehearsal are a matter of taste. Sullivan is outraged by anything that could offend the public, such as Jackie Mason's finger, and he feels personally responsible for keeping off-color material out of American homes. "He may be a purist, but you can't argue with the fact that he knows his audience," Jack Carter said. *Time* magazine called him "the Pope of video," but he is proud of his record.

"One of the requirements of TV is scrupulously good taste. TV goes into millions of homes to family audiences. ... The show has been immaculate." He once said solemnly to his audience, "We want to pledge to you that our show will continue to come into your homes without any embarrassment.... That's our acknowledgment of our appreciation to all of you."

"We watch nightclub performers like hawks." He applied the same vigilance to Esther Williams and Jeanne Crain. In their cases, it was not a matter of cutting but adding material. Both movie stars showed up at dress rehearsal with necklines too low for television. Sullivan instructed the show's wardrobe mistress to cover the cleavage with tulle. Just before they came out onstage, the women ripped out the covering and appeared as voluptuous as at rehearsal. "I immediately relayed instructions to photograph only above their shoulders. I never forgave them."

A favorite editing story of people who work on the show

is told by Julia Meade. She recalls the evening Sullivan took the lion tamer aside one minute before he was going on camera. "Look, we've got to cut you down to three minutes," Sullivan said. "Do you understand?" "Yeah, I understand," the lion tamer replied, "but how am I going to explain it to the lion?"

9

Really Big Shew

"IF I had to name just a few top headliners who were responsible for the biggest moments in our show's history, the list would include Sheila Bond, Billy De Wolfe, Gene Raymond, Johnny Johnston and Bill Tabbert."

The speaker is Ed Sullivan and the year 1951. Today the list has undergone some changes and a dozen highlights stand out in Sullivan's mind. They are the memorable moments he talks about when he reminisces about his television career.

The name of Bob Hope has been prominent on every list of Ed Sullivan's, from 1948 to the present. On September 26, 1948, the comedian made his television debut under unusual circumstances. Earlier in the year comic Al Bernie had agreed to fill in at the last minute when Louis Jordan and his Tympany Five were delayed in traffic coming from Harlem's Apollo Theatre. Sullivan was so appreciative that he promised Bernie another appearance on an evening when his would be the sole comedy spot and he could be presented to the best advantage.

"On the Friday night preceding Bernie's appearance, I

was master of ceremonies at a benefit show at Madison Square Garden. Bob Hope, who was on the bill, said he was very anxious to watch a TV show. 'Tell you what, Ed,' said Hope, 'I've got to go to a West Point dinner at the Waldorf Sunday night, and then rush to La Guardia Airport and catch a plane to the coast. On the way to the airport, if the time schedule works out, I may get a chance to drop in and catch your show.' "

On Sunday night, just before Al Bernie was to go on, the audience suddenly applauded, whistled and stood up. Bob Hope was at the head of the center aisle in the theater, bowing and waving to the people. He walked up to the stage and talked to Sullivan and the audience went wild. This was Bob Hope's television debut and "in those days a movie star in a TV theater was page-one news."

"How much time do you want me to do?" Hope asked the host quietly.

"Get off," Sullivan whispered. "Al Bernie is on next."

Hope joked with the audience. "How do you like this, I am here on the cuff and Sullivan tells me to get off the stage. That's gratitude."

But Hope understood the situation and worked quickly and expertly. He called up Jerry Colonna and Tony Romano of his company for fast bows, and then left the stage to make room for Bernie.

Sullivan had the dancing chorus come on next so Bernie wouldn't have to do his routine immediately after Hope. Ray Bloch went into finale music, and the Toastettes did a two-minute number. Then Sullivan introduced Bernie. When the young comic reached center stage he said, "This is the kind of spot you wouldn't even give a leopard."

"With real courage the kid made a big hit," Sullivan said.

Another comedy high spot in the program's history was provided by a trio consisting of Bing Crosby, Julie Andrews and Phil Silvers.

"I predicated the meeting of these three on an old vaudeville gag: the continuous interruption of a person walking onstage and asking the star in the spotlight 'Now?' "

Phil Silvers began the introduction by saying "one of the great voices of show business, ladies and gentlemen..." At this point Crosby made an entrance and pretended he was being introduced. Silvers acted as if he didn't recognize the singer, ordered him off the stage, and began the introduction over again. Crosby then made his entrance from another part of the stage and asked "Now?" Silvers again ordered him off. He looked at a list of acts in his hand, didn't seem to see Crosby and asked if he was part of a drill team. Finally Silvers introduced Julie Andrews who sang two numbers from *My Fair Lady*. Later they all performed together.

"Each minute was a highlight in itself, and the overall effect of these three stars working together was unforgettable," Sullivan said.

The host's favorite duet took place in 1958 and was "one of the all-time highlights of our show." Sullivan suggested to his old friend Maurice Chevalier that he team up with Sophie Tucker in "I Remember It Well," the tune the Frenchman had introduced in the film *Gigi*. Chevalier found the idea intriguing but had never seen Sophie Tucker sing before. "He went down and watched her work in her club the way a great boxer would watch another great boxer in action. He studied every detail of her act—where she stood, how she read her lines—and decided how to work with her so she would be most comfortable. It was the most masterly preparation of a scene I'd ever seen." When they finally appeared together, "it was a touching moment and great showmanship."

The singing debut of Margaret Truman, made while she was the daughter of the President, provided one of the most exasperating but eventually rewarding moments. Sullivan had been trying to book Miss Truman on the show for one year without success. Then he signed singer Mimi Benzell.

"Our greatest ads are the artists who appear on our show. One performer always leads to another."

Miss Benzell, pleased with the treatment she received on the program, told Miss Truman about it. Next thing Sullivan knew, he was having lunch with Margaret and her manager James Davidson. Ed was certain she would only agree to an interview and was surprised when she asked, "Could I sing on your show?"

The day she appeared was a unique one in the history of the television theater. Secret Service men swarmed through the studio and set up rigid security precautions. "I thought to myself, this is like cops and robbers. It's so silly." Sullivan was frisked by the Secret Service and then later evicted from his own dressing room, which was turned over to Miss Truman for security reasons. The Secret Service then decided that the alley downstairs was potentially perilous to the singer and asked Sullivan to trade rooms with her again.

"When they prowled my room downstairs, discussing whether the fire escape leading to the upstairs dressing room was a potential assassin's route, I couldn't wait for that silly business to be over. But a few weeks later armed fanatics tried to kill President Truman at Blair House in Washington, and I realized it was I who had been foolish."

Margaret Truman was to be paid $2,000 for each of two

appearances but she was such a big hit on the first program that Sullivan called Jim Davidson afterward and raised the fee for the second show to $3,000.

The television audience included the singer's parents, her maternal grandmother and the family cook, all of whom watched from Blair House. For Sullivan the high spot of the evening was President Truman's telephone call to the studio to congratulate his daughter. He then asked to speak to the host and said he was delighted with the way his daughter had been presented. Sullivan had given her a simple introduction instead of a flowery speech and did not mention she was the President's daughter.

One of Sullivan's favorites, as a person and a performer, was the late Charles Laughton, whom the host describes as "a lamb in ogre's clothing." Laughton appeared in 1949 and suggested that he read from the scriptures. "I suppose it would be too much to expect that this benighted, hapless, puerile, infant television, this graveyard of talent, would risk my reading from the Bible."

Sullivan was not only delighted by the idea but insisted that Laughton direct the sequence himself. It was so successful that it resulted in a nationwide Bible-reading tour for the actor.

"Charles always played the part of Captain Bligh off screen as well as on, often to cover his concern for people," Sullivan says.

When the host told Laughton that Frank Fontaine, who was booked for the same show, planned to do a comic imitation of him Laughton became bombastic.

"What! Do you mean to say you have engaged this sniveling lad to impersonate me! I forbid it, I tell you! I have, I assure you, been sufficiently humiliated on this program already. All those blithering, idiotic, half-baked comedians do the same thing—'See here, Mister Christian!' I am sick unto death of it. I tell you Ed, if he goes on, I don't."

Sullivan knew Laughton well enough not to take his ultimatum seriously and persuaded the actor to at least listen. After the comic spoke his first few lines at the rehearsal, Laughton rushed onstage and interrupted. "Enough of this impertinence! Stop, I say!" Fontaine was shaken and Sullivan prepared to apologize to both of them. Laughton halted the host with a gesture, turned to Fontaine and bellowed, "Not like that, young man! Like this!"

"And he proceeded painstakingly to coach Frank in how to mimic Charles Laughton to perfection. Then he turned back to me. 'Ed,' he said, 'when Frank finishes his imitation of me, I'll come bellowing out like a wounded bull elephant and chase him off the stage. That way we may be able to milk another laugh.' He did exactly that in one of the funniest scenes I have ever witnessed."

Another of Sullivan's favorite people was the late Oscar Hammerstein II. The host presented a biography of the lyricist, "The Oscar Hammerstein Story," in two parts on successive Sunday evenings.

"The show achieved greatness and it was because of the utter simplicity and depth of Oscar."

The programs described Hammerstein's eleven difficult years of professional failure, which followed seven years of continuous success collaborating with Otto Harbach and Jerome Kern. During the bad years everything went wrong with his writing and he could not come up with a hit.

"How did a fellow like you, who'd already had tremendous success, take eleven years of bitter and galling defeat?" Sullivan asked.

"I'm married to a wonderful woman. When the lean times are on you, if you haven't got that, you haven't got anything. She always felt I was a success. When I came home at night she made me feel successful, no matter what had happened during the day."

Hammerstein said that the lowest point of his life was when France fell to the Nazis. At the time he had just suggested that "Green Grow the Lilacs" be made into a musical, and although he was later to turn it into *Oklahoma!* with Richard Rodgers, it was turned down then. He had proposed to Jerome Kern that they make an updated musical version of *Carmen* set in Harlem with a prizefighter instead of a bullfighter. This was eventually *Carmen Jones,* but Kern was busy at the time and could not do it. At that moment Paris surrendered. Hammerstein had loved the city and feared he was never going to see a French Paris again. Out of his despondency came the lyrics to the song "The Last Time I Saw Paris," which ended his string of failures.

Hammerstein told the television audience, "I don't sing, I can't dance, I can't tell jokes, but if you like, I'll tell you the lyrics I wrote that day about the wonders of Paris. There is no Folies-Bergère in my lyrics. I wrote about daytime in Paris, the nurses in the park, the children playing, the chestnut blossoms glowing in the springtime sun."

Sullivan said, "He recited the lyrics and our orchestra leader, Ray Bloch, cued his band into underplaying the melody of 'The Last Time I Saw Paris' under Oscar's words. You could have heard a mouse stumble in that theater."

Sullivan considers the Josh Logan story on May 17, 1953, as his single most important program because of its tremendous impact on the public attitude toward mental illness. The Logan story was a biography show that offered highlights from the career of the author-director.

"In the weeks preceding the show when I visited Logan's apartment, it became apparent that Josh was becoming more and more apprehensive about an hour TV show which would recite his stage triumphs. 'I dread the thought of one of those And-Then-I-Wrote sagas,' Josh told me."

Logan preferred doing something that would be of more value to the country. He wanted to talk about his own mental breakdown and his stay in a sanitarium and to tell the audience that breakdowns can be cured. Apparently friends and relatives advised him to steer away from the subject on the television program. It was an unhappy episode in his life, and everyone he knew wanted him to forget about it and not bring the problem into the nation's living rooms.

In the middle of the program Logan was standing backstage next to Sullivan, who asked casually, "How do you like it, Josh?"

Sullivan was amazed when Logan said, "It's horrible. The production is fine, Ed. It's just that all this talk about my success is hollow. I should have gone through with my determination to give a message to the country about mental health. That would have been important."

Logan's voice was intense and embarrassed. "Do you want to do it now?" the host asked.

"I'd love to."

From backstage Sullivan telephoned Ray Bloch and asked him to cut the music at the first possible spot. Moments later the curtain closed and Sullivan stepped in front of the cameras. "Ladies and gentlemen, here is Pulitzer Prize Winner Josh Logan."

Logan took over the stage and addressed the television audience. "This has been gratifying to my ego, but it's not important. As it happens I do have one important thing to tell the country, and I'll tell it quickly. I never got any of the awards I've won until I'd been committed to a mental hospital and released from it. I tell you this because the world is suffering from tension, with the result that many people are crippled by mental breakdowns. The old way of treating them was to hide them in the garden house when people came to visit in warm weather, or lock them up in the attic in winter. You don't have to do either anymore. A lot of people who are disturbed mentally can be cured, just as typhoid, scarlet fever and tuberculosis can be cured. There is no reason why they should go through life bearing a stigma because they have once been mental patients. The proudest memory of my life is that although I had been in the theater a good many years, I never won the Pulitzer Prize until *after* I had been in the sanitarium."

When he finished there was a hush in the theater and then a tremendous burst of applause. "People who were watching Logan's face on their screen at home could see that this was no phony plant. The audience realized that this famous Broadwayite had stripped himself of all pride to tell them something that might help others."

A few weeks later Sullivan received a letter from the chief justice of Pennsylvania's court, Justice Michael A. Musmanno, who enclosed a document he thought Sullivan would be interested in reading. It told of a woman whose broken marriage was the climax in a series of pressures that made it necessary for her to be confined briefly to a mental institution. She responded to treatment and was soon discharged, only to learn that her husband had obtained per-

manent custody of their children under an archaic state law
that reduced former mental patients to the status of second-
class citizens. Her suit to recover custody of her children,
financed by sympathetic neighbors, reached the supreme
court of the state at just about the time that Josh Logan's
story was broadcast. The court ruled that a stay in a mental
institution cannot invalidate a parent's rights as long as a
doctor certifies that the person has been cured.

"The court added, and this was the part that knocked me
out, that its decision was based in part on the statement by
Joshua Logan on 'The Ed Sullivan Show' that he had won
his Pulitzer Prize for *South Pacific* after his release from
treatment at a sanitarium. The woman got her children
back."

Later Sullivan went to Oklahoma City to address an
advertising-club luncheon and told the story. When the
meal was over a doctor came over and introduced himself.
He said he was head of the mental-health program in the
Southwest and there were local repercussions to the Logan
show. For years he had tried to raise money. "The day following your telecast the budget director of my state called
me and told me that I was being given an unsolicited appro-
priation because of what Josh Logan had said on your
show."

"As far as I'm concerned, it was the all-time big moment
on the show," Sullivan says.

Logan's good friend Helen Hayes provided another memorable evening. After the death of her daughter, Mary Mac-
Arthur, Helen Hayes decided that hard work would be the
best therapy and she agreed to be Sullivan's guest. She chose
a scene from *Victoria Regina* where the queen and her family came back to the royal residence after a day's outing,

and someone asks if she is tired from the long ride through London. The queen replies that she felt the strain only once when the police lines had been drawn thin. A group of roughly dressed workingmen broke through, rushed toward her unprotected carriage and stopped about ten feet away. For a moment she feared they were anarchists. Then the toughest-looking man of all called out to her, "Go it, Old Girl; you've done it well."

In a curtain speech Helen Hayes told the audience the reason she had picked the scene. "Someday I'll be making my last appearance. I've lived a singularly blessed life. I've done the things I've loved best with the people I've loved most, the people of the theater. Perhaps before I make my last exit from the stage, you of the American audience, who have been so kind to me, may feel impelled to call out, 'Go it, Old Girl; you've done it well.' "

Sullivan said that everyone was aware she had just lost her daughter and tears ran down the faces of some of the women in the theater. "There followed one of those hushes, which means so much more than handclapping."

Sullivan had his biggest audience when he introduced the Beatles to America on February 9, 1964. According to the Neilsen ratings, 73,700,000 viewers were watching. The program reached more homes in an average minute than any other entertainment program on a single network, before or since.

Teen-age America was gripped by hysteria, and it meant special security precautions had to be taken everywhere. Stand-ins for the Beatles went through a dry run of the arrival from airport to hotel. The actual event was as colorful as anticipated. At an airport press conference the quartet was witty and refreshingly irreverent without being rude.

(Reporter: "How do you find the United States?" Ringo: "Turn left at Greenland.")

Their appearance on the show was their only public performance in New York, and the ticket requests were staggering. Some teen-agers threatened suicide if they were denied admission. Presidents of large corporations had to be turned down after all the seats had been distributed as did Margaret Leighton who had given her two tickets to her maid before deciding she wanted to go herself. Hundreds of policemen were stationed outside the stage door to control the mobs in the street which made Broadway look like New Year's Eve.

It was widely reported that Sullivan signed the quartet after observing at London airport that forty-thousand screaming teen-agers demonstrated for their idols and kept the Queen's plane from taking off. The actual booking was less colorful. The Beatles, though big business in England, had failed to attract any attention in the United States with their records. Capitol then took the group over and tried to give them a new push. The Beatles' manager, Brian Epstein, crossed the Atlantic to talk Sullivan into signing the foursome for three appearances at $8,000. Sullivan booked them despite the advice of associates, who told him not to waste money, since an English act had never made it big in this country. It was many months after their signing that anyone in the United States besides Ed Sullivan and Capitol Records heard about them.

If Beatlemania was ever duplicated on the show, it was in 1956 when Elvis Presley made the first of three appearances for a record $50,000, more money than he has ever paid any single performer before or since. A year before Sullivan had refused to pay $5,000 for one appearance. "I hooted at that kind of money because this was a youngster apparently known only to the Southwest."

Sullivan signed Presley when the host was having an intense Sunday-night rivalry with Steve Allen. Allen had the singer on July 1 and trounced Sullivan in the ratings. When asked to comment, the CBS star said that he wouldn't consider presenting Presley before a family audience. Less than two weeks later he changed his mind and signed a contract. The newspapers asked him to explain his reversal. "What I said then was off the reports I'd heard. I hadn't even seen the guy. Seeing the kinescopes, I don't know what the fuss was all about. For instance, the business about rubbing the thighs. He rubbed one hand on his hip to dry off the perspiration from playing his guitar."

There was a press conference in the studio on the day of Presley's first appearance and Sullivan was impressed by the way the singer handled himself. One reporter asked if he was bothered when silly little girls put their lip imprints all over his new white Cadillac. "I tried to interrupt and help him out, but Elvis disregarded me completely. 'Well, ma'am,' he said politely, 'if it hadn't been for what you call these silly little girls, I wouldn't have had that white Cadillac.' Isn't that a beautiful line for a kid?

"Today Elvis' gyrations are strictly old hat," Sullivan says, though he tried to sign the singer up again last year. He phoned Presley's manager, Col. Tom Parker, and asked about a price. Parker came up with a list of instructions and conditions and after hearing the demands Sullivan said, "Give Elvis my best—and my sympathy," and he hung up.

Presley's appearance on the show served as the inspiration for a scene in the play and movie, *Bye Bye Birdie*. In the fictional plot teen-age idol Conrad Birdie gives one last kiss to a girl on "The Ed Sullivan Show" before he enters the Army. The musical's opening night was one of Sullivan's most unnerving evenings as a celebrity. "We'd heard something to the effect that there was a song about me, but we didn't pay too much attention." The number was a comic hymn to Sullivan sung by Paul Lynde and a chorus. All eyes in the theater focused on Ed and Sylvia Sullivan as the tune reached its deadpan climax with the declaration, "Ed, we love you!" "Sylvia and I sat there with all our friends staring at us. I only wanted the floor to open up and swallow us both."

The story went one step farther than many people would have preferred when fact imitated fiction and as a publicity stunt Gary Lewis gave one last kiss to a girl on "The Ed Sullivan Show" before going into the Army.

Another movie plot in which Sullivan figured prominently was *The Singing Nun,* starring Debbie Reynolds. The film was about Soeur Sourire, the nun whose record of "Dominique" was an international best seller. Sullivan was the only person to get permission to present the Singing Nun in a filmed, taped or live appearance. The Catholic Archdiocese of New York got in touch with its Belgian counterpart, which approved after assurances of the host's good taste. Sullivan brought his television unit into the convent. "Everything went along beautifully until I asked how the check should be made out." He was surprised when the sisters asked for a Jeep instead of money.

"You see, one of our missions in Africa has to make do with an old, battered pickup truck that is falling apart. If you could arrange to ship a Jeep there for us, we would be so very grateful." There was one additional request. "It rains a great deal there and the sisters' habits take a long time to dry once they are soaked. Could you possibly have the Jeep equipped with fiber-glass curtains?"

The relationship between Hollywood and the television show, at its warmest with the film versions of *Bye Bye Birdie* and *The Singing Nun,* was not so cordial when the program first went on the air. There was an unwritten law that motion-picture producers would not contribute to television. Sullivan took a kinescope of the first show to Hollywood in the hope of interesting some of the big stars out there in appearing with him.

"I sent telegrams to everybody I could think of, inviting them to a screening, but none of the stars showed up, only the kids—Robert Stack, Peggy Ann Garner, Shelley Winters —the youngsters who had just come to Hollywood."

Sullivan said that Eddie Cantor and Joan Crawford wanted no part of it, and Al Jolson said, "I'm going to come in when it's established." One producer, who bumped into Sullivan at the Brown Derby restaurant, said, "I can't see any future in TV, Ed. What are you going to do for programming after Gorgeous George, the wrestler, retires?" The only established star he met who recognized the potential of the medium was George Burns.

"Everyone else figured television was a passing fancy like the old Tom Thumb golf game during the depression years." It took six months of effort for Sullivan to break through the Hollywood barrier. He persuaded Nicholas Schenck of M-G-M to give him the television rights to the telephone scene from the motion picture *The Great Ziegfeld.* It was done live on January 9, 1949, with Academy Award Winner Luise Rainer.

During the next year Sullivan presented his first scene from a Broadway play while it was still on the New York stage: Ethel Waters, Julie Harris and Brandon De Wilde in *The Member of the Wedding,* by Carson McCullers.

That year he also presented a scene from the very first play he had ever attended, *Lightnin'.* Victor Moore appeared in the television excerpt, and the cast included a young unknown actor named Robert Horton, who was an extra. Years later, when Horton was the star of "Wagon Train," he met the Sullivans at a party in Hollywood for Lucille Ball and Gary Morton. The actor described that early appearance, "When you introduced the courtroom scene, just before the curtains opened, Ed, I discovered to my horror that the 'judge' wasn't on the bench. So I raced upstairs and found the old gentleman had fallen asleep. I rushed him onstage while Victor Moore glared at both of us." Sullivan checked later and found that Horton was paid $60.

The *Lightnin'* scene originated at the Boston Opera House, and the day before the show Sullivan attended a bazaar in Boston for the benefit of the Marist Nuns. As he left, one of the sisters, Mary Augustine, said, "If anything happens to you, call us. We are known as 'the praying nuns.'" Late that night Sullivan heard from a CBS vice-president in New York informing him of an impending network strike, which would black out the program. Sullivan telephoned Sister Mary Augustine, who said cheerfully, "Don't worry about it, Ed. We'll start praying for you right away. There will be no strike." She was right. At noon Sunday Sullivan was told it was postponed.

Late Sunday afternoon there was another problem. "We were finishing our dress rehearsal and Victor Borge was doing his zany impressions at the piano. Suddenly the lights in the opera house went out. Borge, I thought, had gone too far. On the darkened stage I rushed up to him and said such tomfoolery could easily start a panic."

Borge protested his innocence and said it must be a power failure. He was right. All of the lights in that section of the city had gone out, and it was going to be four or five hours before the repairs could be made, too late for the live show.

"Again I phoned Sister Mary Augustine, and I told her about the new disaster. 'I'm so glad you phoned,' she said happily. 'We'll start praying right away, Ed, and don't you worry at all.'" Sullivan told her that he had to have electrical power by twenty minutes to eight. "I'd now put the Marists on a tight schedule."

"At seven o'clock the Boston Opera House was still in darkness. The streets outside were pitch black. In the pale light of candles our cast was being made up—just in case! At seven thirty not a glimmer of light. Then, at seven thirty-five, five minutes before camera deadline, the lights went on!"

A less eventful but no less memorable dramatic scene took place when Alfred Lunt made his television debut in an excerpt from *There Shall Be No Night,* by Robert E. Sherwood. At rehearsal Lunt was so convincing that for a moment a fellow actor did not realize the star was delivering a line in the script and thought Lunt was talking to him personally. Two other guests on that show were in awe, and after dress rehearsal James Mason said to Raymond Massey: "I'm damned lucky I don't have to follow Alfred in the show." He had stipulated that Sullivan put him on before. Massey laughed. He was going on after Lunt. "I wasn't so wise, but I've got Lincoln's farewell address at

BEHIND MAKEUP. "I once did my show playing a clown. I loved it. Behind makeup I could always be myself, but without it I often feel I am just a baggy-eyed old man."

A HOST OF SULLIVANS. Bewigged with Marty Allen, bewhiskered as the slowest draw in the west and bewildered receiving The Toast of the Town from Soupy Sales.

SEPTEMBER SONGSTERS. Maurice Chevalier, Sophie Tucker, Jimmy Durante.

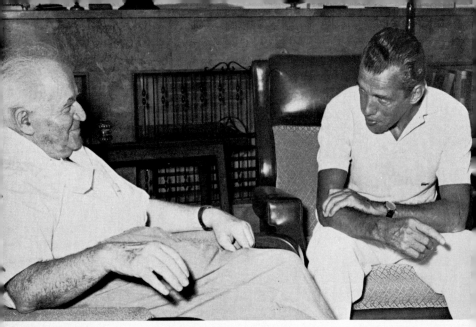

MEDITERRANEAN SYMBOLS. Television interviews range from David Ben-Gurion to Brigitte Bardot.

ROYALTY. Crowning Clark Gable and Myrna Loy King and Queen of the Movies, 1937; Richard Burton, Julie Andrews and Robert Goulet in "Camelot," 1961; Grace Kelly, 1953; Margaret Truman, 1950.

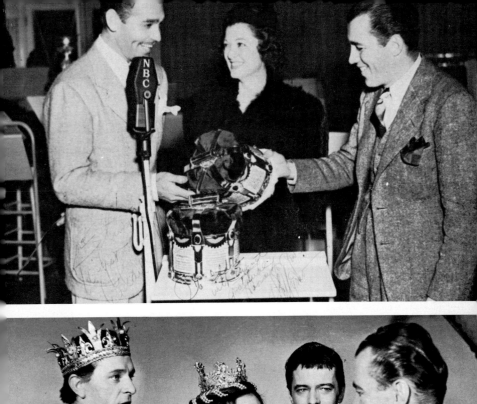

LET'S HEAR IT...AND WE
HEARD. The Beatles, 1964; The
Moiseyev Dancers, 1958.

HELLO, DALI. Salvador Dali, 1961; Pearl Bailey as Dolly Levi, 1967.

HANDS FULL. The right formula for being a good host means soothing one act, being jumpy with another. Marquis Chimps and the Agostinos.

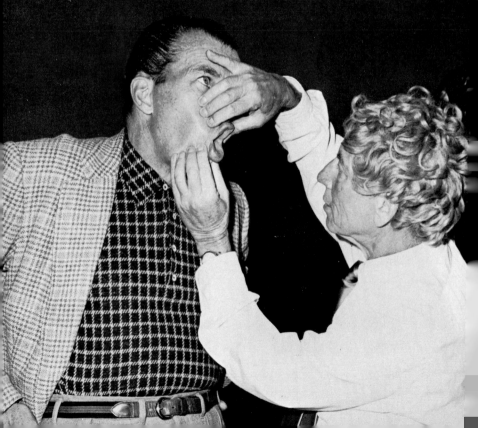

BALLIN' THE JACKS. Three Jacks—Gleason, Paar and Benny—and Lucille Ball bawling.

LESSONS IN SMILING. Phil Silvers, Jack Carter, Harpo Marx.

ED SULLIVAN IS A POINTER ("Rub meat on actors and dogs will do the same," Fred Allen). Fidel Castro, 1960; Walt Disney, 1953; Janet Leigh in a scene from "Bye Bye Birdie," 1963.

RICH VOICES. Barbra Streisand, Maria Callas and George London, Harry Belafonte, Frank Sinatra.

SUPERSTARS. Lauren
Bacall and Humphrey
Bogart, 1951; Gary
Cooper and Louis Arm-
strong, 1955; Sammy
Davis and Fred Astaire,
1955; Dame Margot
Fonteyn and Rudolf
Nureyev, 1965.

THEN AND NOW. Irving Berlin on a Sullivan radio show, 1943; Jerry Lewis, Kathryn Lee, Richard Rodgers, Oscar Hammerstein II, Dean Martin on Sullivan's first television show, June 20, 1948; Bing Crosby in a salute to Irving Berlin, May, 1968.

SERIOUS MOMENTS. Carl Sandburg, 1962 (left), and below, Cole Porter, 1952, and assistant Carmine Santullo at the typewriter in the Delmonico office, 1967.

SOLEMN MOMENTS AND
FAMILY MOMENTS. The Sul-
livans, Archbishop Cooke, Cardinal Spellman at a charity affair,
December 1, 1967—the last photograph taken of the Cardinal; the
Sullivans in St. Patrick's Cathedral after he has been installed as
a Knight of Malta; with grandson
Robert, 1955; with Bob Precht,
Betty Sullivan Precht, Sylvia Sullivan and grandchildren Robert,
Vincent, Carla, Andrew, 1962.

Springfield. Maybe Lincoln can follow Lunt. I certainly wouldn't attempt it on my own."

The scene from *All the Way Home* had a unique transition from Broadway stage to Sullivan show. The play opened in New York on November 30, 1960, to fine notices, but the public did not respond at the box office. After finding only $882 in the till on the second night, producer Arthur Cantor posted a closing notice. Before folding the play officially he asked Sullivan to introduce two members of the cast from the audience. Sullivan had seen the show and liked it, and instead of a brief mention for the stars, he gave an enthusiastic endorsement and urged everybody to rush out and buy tickets. Two hours after the Belasco box office opened on Monday, two thousand dollars' worth of seats were sold and the line was growing. The producers wired Sullivan:

> Our cast and our company thank you. Scores of people in the theater thank you. And indeed hundreds of theatergoers are already thanking you for the generous praise you gave our play on your broadcast last night. Your announcement has already placed a long line of ticket buyers at the Belasco. Amazing box office and telephone activity beginning 10 A.M. this morning has required us to put on third treasurer and telephone girl to handle ticket requests for *All the Way Home*. You have brought an early Merry Christmas to the cast and the backstage crew. Indeed you are a real Santa Claus. God love you. Sincerely.

As a result the show did not close in December, 1960, and went on to win the Pulitzer Prize the following June. The Sunday after the prize was announced, Arthur Hill and Lenka Peterson appeared on the Sullivan stage in a scene from the drama. This victory for the New York theater was

not without its personal headaches for Sullivan. The strong
initial endorsement was contrary to CBS policy. The
company does not permit this kind of plug, considering it
an unpaid commercial. While everyone else was praising
Sullivan, CBS was giving him a discreet reprimand.

Sullivan's major award, of which there are literally hundreds, was the Peabody for his "contribution to international understanding." He received this after touring the
Soviet Union with a troupe of American performers as part
of the United States State Department's cultural exchange
program. It was in 1959 when relationships between the
two countries were first beginning to thaw, and it was the
first time an American variety show performed in the Soviet
Union for the Soviet people. Sullivan spent four weeks in
Moscow and Leningrad and entertained 250,000 Russians.

In Moscow there were nightly performances at Green
Theatre in the Gorky Park of Culture and Rest before an
audience of 10,000 to 13,000 people. The show began with
an overture. The orchestra of forty-three Russian musicians
and one American drummer, conducted by American Elliot
Lawrence, played "America, the Beautiful," and then Sullivan stepped out on the stage. He spoke to the audience in
carefully memorized Russian which he had learned from a
U. S. Army interpreter-teacher: "Thank you, and good evening. My name is Edward Petrovitch Sullivan." His line was
always greeted by tumultuous applause.

The set had red-and-white stripes framed against a sky-
blue backdrop. The red, white and blue motif was carried
through to the finale when the entire cast lined up on the
stage and held small flags above their heads, half American
and half Russian, while Risë Stevens sang "Getting to Know
You." "As she sang the last note, I'd reveal a small Russian

and a small American flag and cross their staffs so the flags were flying together. This always brought a storm of applause."

Sullivan found that the audiences during his Russian tour were the warmest he has ever encountered. "They were incredibly gracious, and their applause was always ear-shattering. It proves that people of different countries have no difficulty in getting along together. Only the politicians can't reach agreement."

One way the Russians expressed their approval was with flowers. Each family that attended the show brought along a small bouquet. At the end of an act, if they enjoyed it deeply, a child representing the family walked up on the stage and presented the flowers to the artist. One night there were forty doctors in the theater from the American College of Surgeons, and just before the intermission Sullivan told his audience about them through an interpreter. "I explained that they were in the country to confer with the great Russian doctors in a mutual undertaking to benefit all the people. The entire audience rose and cheered the American doctors for five minutes and threw up their flowers until the air was filled with hundreds of these tiny bouquets."

During one performance in Leningrad dancer Conrad Buckner injured his left foot while he was performing on stage. Two Russian women doctors who were in the audience phoned for an ambulance and rushed him to a hospital. Buckner came back to the theater on crutches but insisted on appearing in the finale.

"On this particular night I told the people of this city noted for heroism how deeply we appreciated the concern of the two Russian women doctors and how grateful all of us were for the expert care Buckner had received in the hospital. And then I added: 'I told Conrad not to come out in this finale but he said to me, "One does not come to Leningrad—to surrender." '

"Bedlam broke loose in the audience. As the storm of applause died down, again through my interpreter I said to the audience, 'Because of the heroism of your city of Leningrad and because I have been told that each family in this city lost at least one man in the war, I'm certain that there is not a mother in Leningrad—just as there is not a mother in the United States—who ever again wants to send her husband or her son to war.'

"Pandemonium broke loose. The audience surged forward to the orchestra pit. They threw kisses to the Americans onstage and they threw flowers. Women were weeping and dabbing their eyes with handkerchiefs. Some of them threw their arms around Elliot Lawrence. Others patted him on the back. These are the moments that you never forget."

Sullivan did not get the same warm reception from the Soviet officials as he did from the audiences. "We had been promised all kinds of cooperation, but instead all kinds of barriers were placed in our way by self-important bureaucrats trying to make names for themselves." They were having trouble getting their television equipment into the country; despite advance promises, they were denied permission to tape-record some of the show around the city of Moscow; at one point they needed red material, were told there was none and if they wanted to use dye they needed permission from Gosconcert. There were daily meetings with the officials and Sullivan became increasingly angry. One morning the deputy minister of culture asked why he was not smiling. Sullivan said to his interpreter: "Tell the deputy minister that Mr. Sullivan came to his country smiling, but after the treatment he has received here, he does not feel like smiling anymore."

"Driving back to the hotel that night, I was furious. 'If Khrushchev were in town,' I told Sylvia, 'there'd be no problems. This cultural exchange is his program.' A voice from the front seat said unexpectedly, 'Why don't you contact Chairman Khrushchev?' I was taken aback at our interpreter's suggestion. 'How can I contact him?' I asked. 'Isn't he at a Black Sea resort?' 'Just wire the Kremlin,' was the reply. 'He'll have your message in twenty minutes.'

"At the hotel I fired off a vigorous protest wire to Khrushchev, care of the Central Communist Committee, and went to bed feeling much better.

"Next morning, at eight o'clock, my phone rang. The Ministry of Culture was anxious to see me at nine. When I arrived I was greeted by the man who'd been the chief stumbling block. His face wreathed in smiles, he said, 'What would you like, Mr. Sullivan? Everything is yours.' "

Sullivan contacted the Soviet Premier on one other occasion. "When we got back to America, the Russians still owed us about thirty thousand dollars, and the Ministry of Culture seemed indifferent to my requests for payment. I immediately sent a wire to Khrushchev in Moscow telling him what was happening. The next day the Soviet Embassy called from Washington and said that a check had been deposited for us in a United States bank."

Sullivan's travels also took him to Alaska where the highlights included Jill Corey singing "I'm Sitting on Top of the World" while sitting on top of Mendenhall Glacier and George Bruno who did his sway-pole act in Kotzebue above the Arctic Circle in sixty-mile winds and ten-degree-below-zero weather. During rehearsal he climbed the pole with his bare hands and the skin of his palm stuck to the pole. He came down to the ground, bandaged himself and wore fur-lined gloves the rest of the time.

"They paired us up and said, 'If you see a piece of white skin beginning to appear on somebody's face, rush him in-side, because it means it's frostbite.' Here was this aerial act working in the minimum of clothing while the Eskimo women with their papooses stared up in astonishment at the cartwheels he was doing in the air. I think that's one of the most unusual experiences any of us ever had."

Sullivan's travels have taken him around the world, and one performer who has accompanied him often is his good friend Louis Armstrong, whom he considers "one of the incredible giants of show business." Sullivan originated a program from Gian-Carlo Menotti's "Festival of Two Worlds" in Spoleto, Italy, and at the last minute "Satchmo" agreed to appear. The town's hotels were already booked so Menotti invited him to be a guest at his place. Armstrong arrived after a strenuous plane and sixty-eight-mile bus trip which completely exhausted him. At five o'clock in the morning one of the servants in the house woke up Menotti to tell him that Armstrong was gasping for breath and was very sick. Armstrong's personal physician, who travels with him, was unable to speak Italian so Menotti ordered an ambulance and oxygen tanks and alerted the Spoleto Hospi-tal that a very sick patient was arriving shortly. Sullivan was notified and came immediately. As Armstrong was lifted into the ambulance he said to Sullivan, "I'll be all right, Pops."

There was difficulty in diagnosing the illness, which turned out to be pneumonia, but for two days there was a grim deathwatch. Get-well wires came in from all over the world and overwhelmed the town's small telegraph office. After forty-eight hours the crisis ended and Satchmo said to Sullivan, "I guess old Pops is in the clear."

Eileen Farrell was performing in Spoleto in one of Menotti's operas, and she was asked to fill in for the ailing musician and sing jazz with the Armstrong band. Since she was known as an opera and concert singer, no one was sure how she would do. Sullivan says, "She was nothing short of sensational. A few years later, on one of our shows from Las Vegas, I had Eileen and Armstrong sing a duet in commemoration of those grim days and nights at Spoleto."

In Guantanamo Armstrong joined Sullivan at a Christmas show for eight thousand servicemen at a tense time in our relations with Cuba. The audience responded to all the stars in the troupe, but Satchmo was the special favorite. The United Press dispatch out of the Naval base quoted Sullivan: "It was Louis 'Satchmo' Armstrong who was the sentimental favorite. His 'Blueberry Hill,' 'Sleepy Time Down South' and 'Mack the Knife' were showstoppers."

Louis also entertained servicemen with Sullivan in Berlin, and there his incredible popularity was especially apparent. The Sullivans and the Armstrongs had dinner together and then went across the street to a carnival. "It was after midnight and only a handful of people were in the area. Suddenly crowds started gathering. The magic word had gone out that Satchmo had arrived and within fifteen minutes the crowds multiplied to such a fantastic extent that they sent in an emergency call for additional police. All they wanted to do was look at him or touch him."

His personal magnetism was particularly in evidence when he was performing to a group of American soldiers on a drill field at the Army base. "The kids were all sprawled out and he was playing music for them and all of a sudden out of this gay music Louis Armstrong and his band swung into 'Nobody Knows the Trouble I've Seen' and immediately the looks on those GI's faces changed. Now they were thinking of home. They were thinking of their parents. They were thinking, many of them, of their children. And I said to him later, 'Louis, that was a very interesting thing you did there.' He said, 'Well, Ed, it always seems to me that now and then you should have children think. I wanted to make them think.' "

10

The Tempest in the TV Pot

THE feud between Ed Sullivan and Jack Paar began in March, 1961, as a behind-the-scenes dispute over talent fees. With the help of the afternoon New York newspapers it exploded into a national controversy that pushed world news out of the headlines and made the cover of *Life* magazine.

Guests on "The Ed Sullivan Show" were receiving up to $10,000 an appearance while Paar was paying many of the same performers the union minimum wage of $320. The situation had been going on for a while, but Sullivan was not a late-night television watcher then, and somehow it never came to his attention. On Wednesday, March 8, it did.

"I discovered Joan Fairfax performed on the Paar show for three hundred and twenty dollars for one night. I called the Music Corporation of America to find out why."

Joan Fairfax, a Canadian singer, was on his program March 5 and turned up on the Paar show the following night. MCA was technically his agent (though in actual practice he has always been his own) and his contact there, Marty Kummer, also happened to be Paar's agent. Sullivan was irritated to find out that Kummer himself booked Joan Fairfax on the Paar show.

He then learned that Sam Levenson had appeared on the Paar show a number of times and Myron Cohen was booked for March 9. Both men were frequent Sullivan guests and closely identified with the program.

In addition Paar was commenting on air about the difference in talent fees, a gesture not calculated to soothe the Sunday-night host. As Sullivan explained: "Paar, himself, said on camera he didn't understand how he could get stars like Pat Suzuki for three hundred and twenty dollars when she got five thousand dollars on 'The Ed Sullivan Show.' " I was in the odd position of being indicted right in front of Miss Suzuki and the NBC Network as a dope."

Sullivan felt Joan Fairfax had violated her contract's "exclusivity clause," standard in the industry, which forbade her to appear on other programs three weeks before and one week after the Sullivan show without specific permission. Underlying the irritation was his concern for the overexposure of his guests, a common television problem. Stars who appear frequently on other shows are less valuable to him. Viewers don't tune in for an act they're tired of watching or one they know they can see another evening on a different program.

Sullivan did not feel any personal resentment toward Paar. In fact, four years before he helped Paar out when his early-morning television program was canceled on CBS.

"I felt he had gotten a raw deal, especially since I knew he had just bought a new house. So I called Jack and invited him to appear on our show.

"He said, 'Ed, you must be clowning. I've just been fired by CBS, your network. They just won't let you do it.' "

Sullivan said he would take care of that part of it and asked Paar what he earned a week. The answer was $1,500. Sullivan offered $5,000 a show. "It was for as many appearances as I wanted," Paar said, and often expressed his deep appreciation.

"Paar went on our show that Sunday and he began telling this very story to the audience. He was so moved that he started crying and he couldn't finish."

However, the fee situation was a professional, not a personal, matter and Sullivan decided to do something about it. Quietly he notified the talent agents that stars who performed on Jack Paar's program for $320 would get paid the same salary when they appeared on "The Ed Sullivan Show." This did not apply to newcomers or established stars who "talked" with Paar but did not perform. It was the kind of action that goes on behind the scenes and unnoticed almost every day of the year in the communications industry. If Sullivan had been looking for public controversy, he would have contacted the press, but he dealt with the matter in private. As he explained later, "I telephoned the talent agents and the newspapers telephoned me."

The first newspaperman to call was Jack O'Brian who had been tipped off about the situation by a talent agent. O'Brian was then the television columnist for the New York *Journal-American* and one of Sullivan's severest critics. On Thursday, March 9, O'Brian ran an exclusive story which he considered of such little news value that he relegated it to the bottom paragraphs of his column:

> Ed Sullivan today declared war on the Jack Paar show. Nothing personal, Sullivan advised all talent agencies wishing to sell clients to his show. Strictly business. But any stars who perform on the Jack Paar show for $320, the an-

nounced ceiling on Paar show pay, will be paid ONLY $320 if they are booked on the Ed Sullivan Sunday nighter. This declaration of purely business war, Sullivan told all agents involved, has no personal animus.

The initial result of Sullivan's phone calls was Myron Cohen canceling his March 9 Paar appearance when his agent advised him not to show up. "My loyalty lies with Ed because, in great measure, he's responsible for my career."

On Thursday night Paar told his audience about the situation. "Ed Sullivan ... has taken a stand that any performer who comes on this show at the well-publicized figure of three hundred and twenty dollars ... will have to work for that same money on his show. ... I believe he is in violation of Federal law ... right-to-work laws ... anti-trust."

He cited wires of support from Nat "King" Cole, Shelley Berman, Jonathan Winters and Anne Bancroft, and read an open letter to Sullivan, "appearing on the verge of tears— as he often does," as one reporter later described him.

"Dear Ed: I don't think you could have struck any blow that would injure the medium that glorifies you more than the ultimatum you gave television talent today. First of all, I am appalled that you raised the question of money and that you challenge me to pay performers what you pay them. Ed, I don't have money to pay performers. This show is a low-budget freak that caught on because performers want to come on and want time to entertain people without the monkey act and the Japanese jugglers waiting in the wings."

Paar's studio audience laughed and applauded.

He said that answering Sullivan was an emotional strain because of the favor four years before. "Believe me, I'll never forget you helped me when I really needed it. But I've got to level with you, Ed. I made more in those four minutes on your show than I make now in a whole week and I'm kind of a hit now.

"You and I aren't even competing, Ed. As a matter of fact, I'll tell you something. Four years ago when this show started to catch on, NBC was running Steve Allen against you on Sunday nights and they offered me big money to appear on Steve's show to help build a rating against you. But I refused repeatedly because I can't be bought, Ed, nor can my loyalty to a friend. And though now may be a strange time to bring it up I would never do anything to hurt a friend, Ed—four years ago or now.

"If you are able to economically frighten performers off this show, where are you going to find the Bob Newharts who we brought to television, or the next Mike and Elaine you first saw here? Or the Pat Suzuki we found for you? Or Shelley Berman? Where are the Genevieves, the Carol Burnetts, the Earl Grants, the Phyllis Dillers? Believe me, Ed, I want Pat Suzuki to get five thousand dollars from you—nothing could please me more. But it's the three hundred and twenty dollars *here* that made the five thousand dollars possible for so many.

"Ed Sullivan, I am now going to ask NBC for the Sunday-night time eight to nine opposite you at least one week and, Ed Sullivan, I want you to pick the week after you have booked the finest, the best talent that you can get on that show. And that's considerable. It'll be great fun for the audience and we can turn over our entire salaries to the AFTRA [American Federation of Television and Radio Artists] Welfare Fund."

Paar spoke to his audience: "All of you in a way can vote. Watch the show you want to watch, and maybe I'll learn a terrible lesson.... But it would be fun, Ed, wouldn't it? C'mon, old boy!"

The morning papers handled the controversy modestly with small articles on their television pages. "Paar Issues Challenge" was the one-column head for a six-paragraph story in *The New York Times*. The New York *Herald Tribune* and Sullivan's own paper, the *Daily News*, gave the story similar treatment. The afternoon dailies, led by Jack O'Brian, telephoned Sullivan for his reactions as soon as Paar went off the air at 1 A.M. on Friday.

Sullivan said, "I think Paar owes me three hundred and twenty dollars. It's the best show he's had in weeks." As for the rating challenge, "if I were sucker enough to accept, I would get the short end of the stick."

Then he wired Paar, issuing a challenge of his own: "A debate of the issues involved ... tonight, tomorrow or any night mutually agreeable on the 'Tonight' show because the format is more suited to our purpose." He made one stipulation: "So that your national audience can hear each point clearly, let us agree to ban any studio audience."

Paar answered: "Sullivan is most welcome to come on my show. Next Tuesday would be a good night but my studio audience stays. He can't tell me how to run my show. It's my show. He can't change it ... why change the rules for Sullivan? Who is he? ... I don't dictate the policy of his show and I don't want him to dictate the policy on my show.... Sullivan made his hammock and now let him stand up in it. If he fears any discourteousness from the audience I just won't permit it."

Paar sent a return wire:

I am happy to welcome you on the "Tonight" show where you will be given every courtesy we have already extended to President Kennedy, Billy Graham, Vice President Nixon and a host of other guests who have found in our low-budget atmosphere an opportunity to be seen at their informal, relaxed best without limitation of time. However, since none of these mentioned nor any other person who ever appeared requested that people be banned from attending, I feel I must refuse your petition that our meeting be unattended by the live presence of an audience. If the ground rules are to be fair play, I feel any discussion of what will affect the future entertainment of millions of viewers, yours and mine, must be attended, as both of our shows have always been attended, by representatives of the people. Looking forward to seeing you at your convenience, I only hope that your appearance on our show for scale will not ban you from your own. Regards. . . .

Reporters called back Sullivan who said he was willing to go on Paar's show "any night Jack wants me and debate the thing with him. Obviously on my show I can't insult people or do any of the things he does but I'd love to go on his show. . . . I'll debate Jack in his living room with his family on his shoulders. They can be the judges. I'll use his own crews, his own cameraman, even his own makeup man, but I wouldn't like his audience. . . . I am amazed at Paar, who is an expert comedian and performer, for insisting that he must have the help of his studio audience in a debate with me. I don't think that a debate on principles could be aided by an audience that might be persuaded to boo, jeer or cheer. Such demonstrations could be annoying to people listening in. . . . Paar asks for help from his audience. He plays

his audience like an organ.... He cries and they cry. He
chokes up and they choke up.... If he insists on an audience, he's chicken. He doesn't want a debate.... Last night,
for instance, when certain names came up, the audience
howled and booed.... It's like an old Pearl White show.
Jack has got an all-Pearl White audience. If he could control them, I'd be glad to go on his show for the debate. I
would demand my three-hundred-and-twenty-dollar-fee and
I'd turn it over to AFTRA."

Paar responded: "There *will* be an audience. Sullivan will
be welcomed. There was *no* booing or hissing last night. He's
just a bad reporter. I'll be happy to pay him the three hundred and twenty dollars, but what is it he does when he
performs?"

An NBC spokesman said, "Paar has always had a live
audience."

A CBS spokesman said, "This is simply a business matter
and has absolutely nothing to do with personalities. Mr.
Sullivan and Mr. Paar are the best of friends and always
have been."

The afternoon papers put the story on the front page
with banner headlines. "War for Stars Rocks TV" was the
eight-column headline of the *Journal*. The New York *Post*
and the New York *World-Telegram & Sun* broke with lesser
stories in their early editions, but moved the "feud" up to
lead-story status for the middle and late editions. The
Telegram had a five-column headline, "Paar, Sullivan to
Clash in Debate over TV Fees." The *Post* had a headline
across the front page above the name of the newspaper,
"Sullivan-Paar, A New Battle. See page 5." Another story
that afternoon dealt with President Kennedy who had just
urged Premier Khrushchev to cooperate with the United
States in making Laos a completely neutral nation. The

Telegram and the *Journal* both allotted this news one column underneath the television bulletin.

The feud was now the number-one story around the country, and many papers created special departments to handle it, as CBS acknowledged in wires addressed to "TV, City and Sullivan-Paar Desks." Sullivan's telephone almost wore out its bell as reporters frantically competed with each other to get exclusive remarks. The most insignificant comment from either of the principals suddenly became the quote of the day. The attention was incredibly flattering, even hypnotic, and it was easy for a man to lose perspective and take himself too seriously. Even an experienced reporter like Sullivan was not immune to the hysteria. The newspapers encouraged both men to say more and they did.

On Friday, March 10, at 4:23 P.M., Sullivan sent the press a statement of his own and a copy of a telegram he had wired Paar.

The statement: "I am amazed at Jack Paar, who is an excellent comedian and performer, for insisting that he must have the vocal help of the studio audience in the debate which I have suggested. Certainly I am not that formidable."

The telegram:

Dear Jack, Let us direct our debate on important principles to the intellect of your millions of TV viewers rather than to the comparatively small studio audience which nightly responds to your skillful cues with cheers or boos. This could be most disconcerting to me as well as to our TV listeners. I am sure you will agree with me, Jack, that our debate is the important thing rather than the studio sound effects. I'm counting on you to wire your acceptance of this on the basis of good sportsmanship.

Sincerely, Ed Sullivan.

Paar taped an answer which was inserted into the sound portion of that night's show: "This is Jack Paar speaking to you by telephone from my home. I am phoning this message to be played in tonight's repeat show. . . . I think that Ed Sullivan is wrong in a democratic country to give an ultimatum to actors that they could work on one show or another because economically that is what is going to happen. . . . There is going to be an audience every night I am here—Monday, Tuesday, Wednesday. I am not going to change this show for Ed Sullivan." The audience will be the same audience that has requested tickets two months ago. I will see that no one in the next week can get any extra tickets—no page boys, no press photographers, no sponsors. Further, Ed and I will walk out together. There will be nobody to speak before the other. The third thing, I insist humbly that Ed speak first and last.

"Fourth, I suggest that Ed bring his own moderator, his closest friend, his lawyer, anyone he wants to bring. . . . I'm perfectly willing to go on Sullivan's show before an audience or without an audience . . . on only one provision—and that is that some time be given to the issues that he has raised. I don't want to be given four minutes and then have eight acrobats come on in the middle of the discussion."

Later Paar said he had finally found someone "more incoherent, more emotional and more nutty than I am." Sullivan replied, "That's impossible."

Paar said, "I've learned long ago not to talk to the press because I'm a maverick in this business. I'm not terribly talented but I'm different. I will be misquoted. They pull every old picture out of the file as they have in the New York tabloids today and in every picture I'm either talking or have my mouth full of food or some ridiculous shot.

But this is how the press, the tabloid press of New York, operates. I just want you to be aware of it. Ed Sullivan is a columnist and if you attack a columnist and say anything about a columnist, even gently correct him, it's like shooting a cop in New York. Everyone comes down on your head."

Sullivan replied, "Actually I thought the pictures of Paar in the newspapers were the finest I've ever seen."

On Saturday morning, March 11, the entire front page of the New York *Mirror* had the headline "Sullivan Paar Feud, Trade TV Challenges. Story on page 3." *The New York Times* wrote "Sullivan had set a fast pace after taking the lead. . . . Sullivan turned on the pressure . . . it was the second time this winter that Sullivan had brought a crowd to its feet." The story was on the sports page and was about Tom Sullivan of St. George High School in Chicago, who was in a track meet. He was the Sullivan who received the most attention that morning in the *Times*. The feud was on the television page. The front page was devoted to Laos, the Congo and Angola.

The Saturday afternoon papers had a new development to announce and they splashed it across the front pages with the same eight-column headlines as the day before. "Sullivan Says Yes, Goes on Paar's Show Monday," said the *Post* and "Sullivan Yields to Paar on TV Debate Terms" was the way the *Telegram* put it. The *Journal* wrote "TV Stars to Debate Monday," giving it five more columns than their story about Elizabeth Taylor's recovery from her near-fatal illness. Sullivan agreed to the debate after NBC-TV Vice-President Jerry Danzig assured him that "the audience will not be rigged." Sullivan explained to newspapermen that he had been careful "because this is an emotional man who feels the whole world is against him—look at his many fights and feuds."

Sullivan wired his acceptance:

Relying on assurances from NBC-TV and Paar about the debate which I have proposed, I will waive my insistence on the elimination of Paar's studio audience at the video taping of our debate. I have been told that there will be no audience rudeness such as disturbed Chicago newspaperman Irv Kupcinet and the New York *Herald Tribune*'s Hy Gardner when they were invited to his show for a question-and-answer session.

The papers now polled entertainers to get their reactions to the feud. Phyllis Diller was in the awkward position of having an upcoming booking on the Sullivan show on March 26 with a commitment to appear on the "Tonight" show the following evening. "I feel like turning around and leaving town," she said. Jackie Gleason wired Paar and invited him to appear on his next program guaranteeing a payment of $320. One reporter even queried a spokesman for the anti-trust division of the United States Attorney's Office in New York. The response: "If Paar wants to come down to make a complaint he's welcome to do so."

The discussion now turned to the selection of a moderator. Walter Cronkite, Douglas Edwards and John Daly were all considered and rejected as possibilities. James Hagerty's name was proposed and an NBC executive vetoed that idea. "Why should we give all that publicity to ABC?" he said. Ed Sullivan said that his two suggestions, Hugh Downs and Donald A. Connolly, head of AFTRA, had been rejected by the Paar faction.

Paar responded quickly: "I never even *heard* of the suggestion. I never turn down anybody. It's not up to me to

choose the moderator. I told Ed in front of my television
audience that he could pick the moderator and make the
ground rules. He can bring Dorothy Kilgallen if he wants
or Walter Winchell. Anybody. I couldn't care less who he
picks.

"I will do anything Ed Sullivan wants to do. My only
condition is that there be a TV audience. Mr. Sullivan
invited himself on my show. He cannot change my show.
I resent his snide reference to my audience that I play them
like an organ, that they're unruly. In all the years I've been
doing the show they booed only once and with good cause.
That was the night an America firster came on and said
we ought to drop a bomb over Red China.

"But if Ed is so afraid of coming before my audience,
I've said I would be glad to go on his show tomorrow night
and battle it out in front of his fans, if he has any fans. He
said I was 'chicken' when I refused to debate without an
audience. Well he'd better be ready Monday night."

Ed Sullivan said, "The issues have become so garbled,
so clouded, I think they should be straightened out. Let
the public know the issues."

On Sunday morning the New York *Mirror* became the
first to pose a question which others would echo in the
following days. Their front-page headline: "TV Battle
Monday: Is It A 'Stunt'?"

On Sunday, March 12, Bennett Cerf was chosen as moderator. He said he first heard about it "when I was just
climbing out of the shower Sunday morning. I guess I said
Yes when I was still wet. . . . I know I like both Ed and
Jack, and I'm reasonably sure they like me." Sullivan spent
the day preparing his regular Sunday-night program and
meeting with his lawyer and with his producer, Bob Precht,

to formulate prepared comments for the debate. Reporters passed the day at the studio waiting for fresh bulletins.

Jack Paar said, "I'll guarantee it will not be a friendly debate."

Sullivan's response: "I don't want to walk in the studio with him. I don't want to shake hands with him. I don't want to sit at the same table or desk with him."

Paar said, "I don't want to see Sullivan before the debate. I don't want to give him a chance to soften me up, though I doubt he could anyway."

On Monday *The New York Times* paralleled the "two big bouts" competing for attention on the airwaves that night. The second was the heavyweight championship fight between Floyd Patterson and Ingemar Johansson which was being broadcast on radio. The article said that the Paar show "is normally televised in what NBC calls 'living color.' But some observers have asked if this time it will come out livid. Yesterday the participants agreed on Bennett Cerf as a referee or moderator. Whether the 'What's My Line' panelist can avoid puns and take the matter seriously remains to be seen."

That day Bob Precht and Paul Orr, producers of the two shows, and NBC Vice-President Jim Stabile met in Bennett Cerf's office to make arrangements for the debate. At Paar's request reporters were to be barred from the audience and watch the taping on a monitor in a private room. Sullivan would speak first. Paar would present his rebuttal, then Sullivan would have another chance to speak. Cerf, as moderator, would open and close the half-hour session. Afterward Paar and Sullivan would exit separately. Then Hugh Downs, Paar's announcer, would take over the show for the remaining period. Paar had agreed there would be no mention of the debate on the program which followed.

Precht and Orr left Cerf's office and did not make any statements to the crowd of reporters waiting outside. Cerf did. "They're going back to confer with their principals now. We've spent the last hour deliberating about how much time each one would get—setting up the ground rules, so to speak. That's all. We don't want to build this into a Kennedy-Nixon debate. It's a problem that doesn't belong to the public at all. Nothing has been agreed upon. The plans may change even before the show goes on."

Sullivan understood it would be a debate, not a discussion, and continued preparing his remarks. At 2:30 P.M. Paar's office notified him that Paar insisted on a discussion. Sullivan refused.

He wired the press:

Jack Paar, through his representatives, has just called off tonight's debate. Paar simply has welched. As a matter of record I challenged Paar to this debate last week. He specifically accepted the debate. This morning in the presence of moderator Bennett Cerf at Random House, Paar's attorney, James Stabile, acknowledged that the word "debate" means that each side in turn presents his argument and that the first speaker ends the debate with rebuttal. The other day Paar in newspapers insisted that I speak first and that I speak last. I agreed to this. Paar has now said that he will not appear unless I agree that following the debate we will have a discussion. Obviously after the debate I'd have nothing to discuss with Paar and there would be no subject open to discuss. I am ready to go on tonight and debate. If Paar wants to change his mind before 4:00 P.M. I will go on. Paar can now put up or shut up and his deadline is now 4 P.M. I have no further comment.

The wire was transmitted at 3:28 P.M. NBC responded with a lengthy statement saying, in essence, that "Sullivan bowed out."

Sullivan said, "The welcher's deadline expired at four o'clock. Paar simply has welched. . . . I refused a discussion because I have nothing to discuss. . . . When Paar was notified he immediately choked up and started to pull his crying bit. You know the old vaudeville routine of bringing your wife and children onstage when your act stinks. . . . He's overflowing with emotion. Now he wants to get into a loveseat with me after the debate. He told me I could make the ground rules and now he's trying to tell me what they'll be. . . .

"Paar is a welcher. He is a hell of a shadowboxer but I think he chokes up when he realizes the time has come to stand up and debate. I was all set. My makeup man was already here in my office but Paar realized that he didn't have a leg to stand on. . . . My wife and I turned down front-row seats to the Patterson-Johansson fight in Miami Beach for this. . . . I stayed here. . . . That's the thing that really burns me up."

Paar said, "Sullivan has backed out. He would not agree to a free and open discussion of the issues, the only condition I made and the only democratic way of clearing up the whole mess. Heck, I agreed to everything else: that he choose the moderator, that he bring his own makeup man, that he have the use of the teleprompter, that he stand centerstage, that there be only three-quarter length shots of him, that there be no reaction shots, that he appear first and last. Obviously he was looking for an out."

When Bennett Cerf was notified that the debate was off, he was dismayed. "Oh, my God! When they left my office this morning after arranging the ground rules, they were still arguing over whether there should be a discussion after the debate." Then he closed the subject. "I have a book-publishing company to run," he announced.

Groucho Marx said, "I have worries of my own. I might have to give up my own NBC Thursday-night show if we can't get more cigars out of Cuba."

The afternoon papers ran eight-column headlines which *Time* magazine later described as "blacker than the Congo." ("And why not?" *Time* asked. "The combatants, after all, were a lot more famous than Gizenga or even Adlai Stevenson.")

That night announcer Hugh Downs told the Paar show audience that it was about to witness an unusual and important television event. Then Paar stepped forward and opened a fifteen-minute monologue by saying, "Ed Sullivan has proved to be as honest as he is talented."

He said he "never felt more melancholy" and was "disappointed in Sullivan as a man." He asked MCA to release him from his contract because the agency had not bothered to get in touch with him after the feud began. ("Jules, don't take any more of my money.")

"I think I'm as normal and decent a person as you'll find in show business. . . . I do not enjoy what I am about to do to Mr. Sullivan." What he was about to do was call him "The Masked Marvel" and tell the audience Sullivan asked for a teleprompter and "any idiot can read a teleprompter."

"He is afraid to appear on the show—not that he would be murdered but that he would commit suicide in front of an audience. . . . Everybody looks more interesting here, and if you had been here, Ed, you might have looked more interesting for the first time."

Paar addressed his audience: "Why would you be rigged? ...Mr. Sullivan implies that you are rigged. I wonder how those tennis players and golf players and those movie actors who stand up in the audience...I wonder if they just happen to be there.... Sullivan perhaps rigs his audience.

"A debate means we discuss it, that we argue if you like, that we ask each other questions, that I present a few little things to Mr. Sullivan about his past operations, about how financially he has run that show, about the people he has conned, about the way he has used his column to beat people over the head who would not come on his show. This is what I wanted to discuss because this is what is behind it all....

"I am not going to fool around much longer about how I feel about Mr. Sullivan because he has made a very difficult decision performers must decide, a loyalty which is unnecessary. I don't want my friends to have to decide between Ed Sullivan's money or my friendship or loyalty or enthusiasm for them.... They are apparently going through a heck of an experience and I do not want them to have to decide such a very important decision.

"Ed Sullivan is a liar. That is libel. He must now sue and he must go to court—and not like Winchell and Hoffa who sue just to save their face. The public is going to insist you go to court and under oath, I repeat, Ed Sullivan, you lied today."

Ed Sullivan watched from his Delmonico apartment and was relaxed during the broadcast. He often paid more attention to his poodle Bojangles than to his television set and it was difficult to catch Paar saying "any idiot can read a teleprompter" because Bojangles had a ball and was jumping two feet in the air in front of the screen. When Paar called him a liar, Sullivan roared with laughter. The charge was "not only vulgar but completely untrue" though he had no intention of suing for libel. "As someone once said, never sue if someone calls you a liar because he's liable to prove it. I've told a lie from time to time. Who hasn't?

"I couldn't go up against Paar in this 'discussion' business he insisted upon. He'd just love to get into a discussion where he can heckle, make interruptions, irrelevancies, anything to make a point. . . . In a debate you make your point and you can underscore it. In a discussion it's easy to obscure the point by getting involved in irrelevancies. . . . This is the kind of situation that fits the talent of a comic. . . . I'm a newspaperman and interested in the facts. . . . I've never pretended to be a comedian, quick with the gag lines. Paar's a very good comic. In any fifteen-minute discussion he could kill me. . . . I won't tell a lie about Paar. Despite all the smoke screen and publicity from NBC, this fellow walked out on the debate."

Paar was in seclusion at his home in Bronxville, New York, and refused to talk to reporters or reply immediately to Sullivan's remarks.

Life was at work on their story which would be on the stands the following week. The cover of the magazine would depict an Ed Sullivan and a Jack Paar puppet fighting each other. Inside the puppets acted out episodes in the dispute with the actual quotations of the principals as captions. "Puppets Parody Fly-Weight Feud" was the title

of the article. According to *Life,* "The Punch and Judy
show makes as much sense as did the real-life brawl."

On Tuesday morning the New York *Mirror* front-paged
the story again but *The New York Times* printed a critical
editorial by Jack Gould entitled "Highly Distasteful
Brawl":

> At a time when the rest of the world is concerned over
> grave issues, the United States presents the spectacle of two
> grown men, each enjoying an annual income well up in six
> figures, regaling millions of their fellow citizens with alloca-
> tions and innuendos about each other. . . . The emergence of
> the dispute emphasizes the almost incredible pressures that
> are a daily part of the TV life. The fierceness of the constant
> fight for survival in video is indicative of how the law of
> the jungle devours many otherwise sensible people and di-
> rectly affects what the public sees.
>
> Hours of time on television and eight-column streamers in
> the newspapers for the Messrs. Paar and Sullivan? If the
> people of the Congo think we have gone back to the playpen
> they can't be blamed.

The New York Times editorial had an impact at the
Delmonico Hotel and at the CBS executive offices, and
there was agreement to call a halt to the controversy at
this time. On Tuesday, March 14, at 2:05 P.M., CBS sent
out a wire with Ed Sullivan's final statement.

> Before planing today to Miami to fulfill a long-standing
> engagement to emcee a charity show for crippled children Ed
> Sullivan issued this statement: "Paar's intemperate display
> on his show last night indicated how wise we were in insisting
> on a formal debate from which he withdrew. Paar proved
> last night that he did not intend at any time to debate the
> issue and that his demand for a discussion instead of debate
> only was a cloak for exactly what he did last night: name-

calling, a shocking indulgence in personalities and a continued willful distortion of the true issue.

"For thirteen years I have attempted to present wholesome entertainment for the entire family. I stand on this record. This controversy, as Paar's behavior proved last night, is clearly a misuse and an abuse of the airways and has become objectionable to the public. Consequently I will have nothing more to say on this subject."

On Tuesday night Paar said he had wired Sullivan offering to "welcome you on my show to say what you want, stand where you want, speak as long as you wish without interruption. . . . If you prefer we will accept your remarks on video tape. . . ." On Wednesday night Paar said, "I have lost the battle to Mr. Sullivan in the daily papers. . . . Ed Sullivan and I could never be friends after what went on." A few minutes later Hugh Downs questioned the last statement. Paar said, "You want me to retract that? I'll retract it."

Ed Sullivan remained silent and did not answer the charges. He resisted all attempts to elicit new comments from him.

Then, in 1967, he was having lunch at the Colony restaurant with a reporter and a researcher from *Time* magazine, which was doing a story on him. The reporter asked about many of the people in his past including Paar. The only personal contact Sullivan himself had during the intervening years was to fill a ticket request for Paar when his daughter wanted to see the Beatles show. Sullivan's memory was of a man who had returned a favor by insulting him in public. At the Colony he did not weigh his remarks carefully before speaking or think about how his words would look in print.

Time magazine wrote in the October 13 issue: "Such is his relative benignity that the worst he can say for his old competitor Jack Paar is that he is a 'thoroughly no-good son of a bitch. That's spelled s-o-n ...' "

Paar responded in print and on television. *Time* magazine put his answer in their "Letters to the Editor" section with the head "And Now Here's Jack!" "In your article on 'Variety Shows' [Oct. 13], Ed Sullivan referred to me as a 'thoroughly no-good son of a bitch.' Mr. Sullivan always had trouble with the truth and I have a birth certificate to prove him false again. Furthermore, I state as a sworn fact that Ed Sullivan's office has called my agent on at least four or five occasions in the past year to get me to do a television special in cooperation with his company; and are you ready for one of the subjects that he chose for me? The Vatican. I declined."

Paar made his on-the-air reply on Lee Bailey's half-hour interview program "Good Company" on October 26. "Ed is not noted for his use of language. It's not his strong point. His strong point is singing and dancing and we all remember and love Ed when he used to put his feet over the footlights and sing 'Over the Rainbow.' ... I don't know why he said it unless he was trying to prove at his age some kind of manhood. ... NBC has its peacock and I think that CBS now has its cuckoo. ... Ed Sullivan is the best thing on his show. ... It's probably the miracle of all of show business. ... Who can bring to a simple English sentence such suspense and mystery and drama? ... Who but Ed Sullivan can introduce a basketball player with the reverence once reserved for Dr. Schweitzer?"

Afterward Sullivan said, "I regret having said it. It was a flare-up. I wish we could turn the calendar back. I wish it hadn't occurred. You just shouldn't pop off like that. . . . Paar is a damn talented guy." Then he wrote Paar a personal letter and expressed the same sentiment. Paar wrote a warm letter back and the feud was over again.

Before and after the "flare-up" Sullivan said privately that he doesn't want or need the kind of controversy that goes with a public feud. "Nobody gains from a thing like that."

Nobody except the press. Television feuds sell papers. On March 15, 1961, Sullivan and Paar were no longer news. The afternoon dailies dropped them from page one, but the *Journal* tried to fill the gap by developing a new story: "Bing vs. Garry: Carol is Prize" was the front page headline. "Rivalry of Garry Moore and Bing Crosby for the appearance of singer-dancer Carol Lawrence on their TV shows wound up in a Supreme Court trial today. . . ."

11

Four, Ten and Eleven Letter Words

On a Sunday afternoon in 1967 Ed Sullivan was in his dressing room with an advance copy of a national magazine which would be on the newsstands a few days later. He was reading a profile of himself which contained critical remarks he had made about some people. He was in good spirits because the article was flattering, but he was reflective as well as jovial: "You know, tonight around midnight Sylvia's going to turn to me and say, 'Why did you have to start something again?'"

Ed Sullivan has made headlines in a number of celebrated feuds that have spanned two decades of television. Today he can hardly recall what some of them were about, but at the time they aroused anger, and they were good copy.

FRANK SINATRA

Today Frank Sinatra is his friend, and Nancy and Frank, Jr., have made many appearances on the show. The relationship was less cordial at another time.

The two men started off as friends. During World War II Sinatra helped entertain wounded servicemen in Ed Sullivan's hospital shows and joined his war-bond drives. When Westbrook Pegler and Lee Mortimer attacked Sinatra, and Sullivan stood firmly in the singer's corner, the friendship was cemented. Sinatra sent Sullivan a wristwatch. The enclosed card referred to the joke that the singer did not have any blood and had to support himself onstage by holding onto the microphone: "Ed, you can have my last drop of blood."

After the war they saw very little of each other, but the friendship was deep-seated and didn't require daily contact. Then in the spring of 1955 the situation changed. Ed Sullivan made a $32,000 deal with Samuel Goldwyn for thirty minutes of the motion picture *Guys and Dolls* starring Marlon Brando, Jean Simmons, Vivian Blaine and Sinatra. Goldwyn wanted the television plug to help push an expensive film, and Sullivan wanted the box-office names as an audience draw for his show.

Sinatra reacted to the deal with anger and said he would not do anything for the Sullivan show unless he was paid $25,000.

When the press asked Sullivan to comment, he said that he hadn't talked to Sinatra but found it hard to believe he had been attacked. He said the contract was signed with Goldwyn, who was solely responsible for delivering the thirty minutes of film. Meanwhile the newspapers played up the story and it became page-one news. Sullivan considered it "a silly little thing" which was being magnified during a dull stretch in entertainment news, but suddenly it turned into "a vicious attempt to smear me and the show."

Sullivan's lawyer, Arnold Grant, advised him to make a vigorous and definitive statement. Sullivan spoke to Walter Pidgeon, then president of the Screen Actors Guild, who said that a recent ruling to prevent newspaper personalities from using movie celebrities on television without pay was directed not at Sullivan, who had always paid performers, but at Hollywood columnists. Sullivan took out an ad on the entire back page of the Hollywood *Reporter* and in Hollywood's *Daily Variety* with an open letter to Pidgeon:

Dear Walter:

Let us waive the important fact that the SAG ruling actually was directed at other columnists, not me. Let us waive, for the moment, the fact that I haven't talked to Sinatra in some years; and let us overlook the fact that Sinatra, regularly trounced by us when he becomes part of the rival network's "spectacular," hardly qualifies as an impartial or disinterested witness.

What I particularly resent is Sinatra's reckless charge that "Toast" does not pay performers. To date we have paid out over $5,000,000 in salaries and, incidentally, rendered substantial benefits to motion pictures, motion-picture artists, studios and theater operators.

If Sam Goldwyn approached Sinatra, that hardly is my concern or problem. Certainly I never approached Sinatra. My negotiations with Mr. Goldwyn involved an offer by me to pay a substantial sum of money, $32,000 covering studio technical costs, to represent, on film, thirty minutes of *Guys and Dolls* as an exclusive preview.

Sincerely,
Ed Sullivan

P.S. Aside to Frankie Boy: Never mind that tremulous 1947 offer: "Ed, you can have my last drop of blood."

Four days later Sinatra ran an answer in the same coast trade papers: "Dear Ed, you're sick. Frankie. P.S. Sick, sick, sick!" The ads brought more headline stories around the country.

Four months later the feud ended dramatically. "When an automobile crash put me in the hospital in 1956, Sinatra was one of the first stars to offer to substitute for me on our Sunday-night show. When Frank learned that Red Skelton already had volunteered to act as master of ceremonies, he insisted on appearing anyway."

Sinatra refused to be paid for the appearance.

NAT "KING" COLE

Ed Sullivan and Nat "King" Cole had been good friends until 1961. On January 26 of that year Cole was off the Sullivan show "in a dispute over material," as newspapers put it. The *Journal-American* wrote: "Nat wished to sing a brand-new song whose recorded version will be released next Monday. Sullivan and his staff demurred on the basis the song was being sung only to publicize its sale as a recording." "How does a standard become a standard if it's not introduced by people like me?" Cole said at the time. And he came forth with a less discreet blast in the July issue of *Cosmopolitan* magazine. Cole never returned to the program and instead made numerous appearances with Jack Paar.

Later Sullivan learned that Cole was seriously ill and he wished him luck on the air and urged viewers to send the singer telegrams and letters. Cole received 600,000 messages and he was moved deeply. "I've got to do something for Ed," he said. "When I'm over all this sick business I'll make my first public appearance on his show. I think

that would be nice. I think that would straighten everything out." Cole died before that could happen.

When his widow, Maria Cole, decided to resume her
singing career, the showcase for her comeback was "The
Ed Sullivan Show."

HEDDA HOPPER

Hedda Hopper was signed by NBC for a television special
on Sunday night at eight o'clock in competition with the
Sullivan show. Because of her influence as a motion-picture
columnist she was able to get Hollywood celebrities for the
union minimum and lined up a low-budget program with
box-office names. Although this was to be a one-time show,
it was obvious that NBC would schedule her against Sullivan regularly if she drew a big audience.

One of the guests she announced was Charlton Heston, who had appeared on the Sullivan show not long before for $10,000. Sullivan publicly criticized Hedda Hop-
per's tactics, and his remarks resulted in an acid exchange
of statements which received front-page attention. He also
complained to AFTRA and sent a formal protest to Ronald
Reagan, who was then president of the Screen Actors Guild.

"Reagan declared that he never received my letter. I
always was convinced that he did because this item appeared in Hedda Hopper's column: 'Ronald Reagan and I
had a great laugh at that letter from that New York columnist.' In a letter dated July 8, 1966, Reagan wrote to
me: 'I repeat that I knew of no item in Hedda's column
but cannot say that no such item appeared. I have just
never been a reader of the Hollywood columns.' That statement—that a Hollywood actor never read the Hollywood
columns—is incredible."

Nevertheless, Sullivan's criticism of Hedda Hopper was effective. Heston and others withdrew from her program and new stars decided not to sign. The episode was awkward for the *News*, Sullivan's own newspaper, because Hedda Hopper was their Hollywood columnist while her rival, Louella Parsons, who worked for a competing syndicate, backed Sullivan. In addition, the situation was complicated because some critics said Sullivan was attacking the very tactics which had made his own show a success in the earliest years.

ARTHUR GODFREY

Ed Sullivan and Arthur Godfrey have probably talked to each other face to face less than half a dozen times, but a "feud" between the two men existed for many years. It ended in 1967 when Godfrey accepted Sullivan's invitation to appear on the Dec. 24 program. The beginning was more dramatic.

In 1953 Arthur Godfrey fired Julius La Rosa from his program while on air, and the story was page-one news all over the country. The singer had been getting $1,000 a week from Godfrey but Sullivan signed him immediately for a "television comeback" at $30,000 for six appearances. With his news sense he knew that La Rosa would attract a large audience for his own program.

That first evening the host did not tease his audience by delaying the singer's appearance but said as soon as he came onstage: "I know what you're waiting for. Ladies and gentlemen, Julius La Rosa." Any hard feelings on Godfrey's part may have been intensified by the fact that Godfrey's mother, one of Ed Sullivan's biggest fans (who has often prepared homemade jam for the host), was sitting in Sulli-

van's audience that night "screaming and applauding" for
Julius.

Sullivan was following his instincts as a showman. He
anticipated and got one of the highest ratings in the history of his show. He had no animosity toward Godfrey, not,
that is, until 1954, and then over a plane. In January of
that year Godfrey was charged by the C.A.A. with buzz-
ing the control tower at Teterboro Airport. Sullivan was
"shocked" and assumed Godfrey would apologize. Instead,
Godfrey suggested on air that Fred M. Glass, director of
aviation for New York's Port Authority in charge of Metropolitan airports, was "picking on me, because I'm a big
name. Probably he wants to run for governor of New York
State."

Sullivan became incensed and started his own investigation which "after the most exhaustive probe" resulted
in a *Daily News* column under his by-line on January 16,
1954. The title was "The Godfrey Case."

> On November 1, 1949, the control tower at Washington,
> D.C., National Airport ordered the flier of a P-38 to make
> a left turn and circle the field. He disobeyed, violated the
> traffic pattern, crashed into an Eastern Airlines DC-4 and
> killed 55 people, including veteran airline pilot Captain
> Charles Hazelton, Tammany leader Mike Kennedy, New
> Yorker cartoonist Helen E. Hokinson, Massachusetts Repre-
> sentative George J. Bates and 51 others.
>
> So the flippancies of Arthur Godfrey, in answering charges
> of reckless operation of his DC-3, taking off from Teterboro
> Airport, are shocking. Godfrey is 50, hardly the age of a
> hot-rodder.
>
> The Teterboro control-tower log gives a sinister pattern
> to Godfrey's flippancies. I asked the C.A.A. if, following
> the hairbreadth escape of control-tower personnel, Godfrey

had radioed an apology or explanation to the men he had endangered.

"The control tower contacted Godfrey immediately," said the C.A.A. spokesman. "They asked him if the plane was out of control, or in trouble."

"What did Godfrey reply?"

"No, that's just a normal Teterboro takeoff," said Godfrey.

That contemptuous reply to the control tower best illustrates Godfrey's major weakness, his inability to apologize. But this time it has caught him in the backfire. . . . Godfrey is sensational on a TV screen. But there's no place for sensationalism in flying. That is for the birds.

Sullivan pointed out later that Godfrey did not challenge any statement in the column. The pilot's license to fly was suspended by the C.A.A. on March 16, 1954. It was reinstated September 17, 1954.

In 1955 Godfrey fired singer Marion Marlowe and Sullivan signed her up too for $3,000 an appearance. "It's nothing personal against Godfrey. If they'd fire him, I'd try to sign him up too," Sullivan said at the time. Godfrey's reply: "I'd certainly accept the offer."

INGRID BERGMAN

On July 18, 1956, Ed Sullivan announced that Ingrid Bergman, absent from the United States for seven and a half years, would return to this country that fall to appear on his show. At the time the actress was in London making *Anastasia,* her first American motion picture since her widely publicized romance with Roberto Rossellini. Sullivan said that he was flying to London to make final arrangements for the appearance. He returned to the United States with a clip from the motion picture provided by Twentieth

Century-Fox, which was eager to publicize the film by exposure on the Sullivan show.

On July 24 Ingrid Bergman told a London interviewer there was no truth to the story about her scheduled television appearance. She said that Sullivan was going to use filmed excerpts but "there never was any question of my going to the States with him."

On July 29 Sullivan made the following statement on his Sunday-night program:

"Now the film has been made. Now over there it seemed to me that this thing should be left up to the American audience because you decide everything. I was planning to use the film on our show at some time: she doing a scene with Helen Hayes.

"Now I know that she's a controversial figure, so it's entirely up to you. If you want her on our show, I wish you'd drop me a note and let me know to that effect. And if you don't, if you think it shouldn't be done, you also let me know that too, because I say it's your decision and I'd like to get your verdict on it.

"I think the lot of you think that this woman has had seven and a half years—you know she's had seven and a half years of time for penance. Others may not think so, but whatever you think, it would clarify because everybody's newspaper has called up this morning. When I came into the office they wanted to know what this decision had been on the Ingrid Bergman appearance on our show and I told them what I told you; it's entirely up to the public."

A great deal of copy followed this controversial announcement. *Newsweek* magazine reported in August that at that time the mail count was 5,826 for Miss Bergman and 6,433

against. Jack Shanley devoted an entire Sunday column in
The New York Times to a criticism of Sullivan's speech,
and syndicated columnist Hal Humphrey ended up his
blast by asking "Incidentally, when is Ed Sullivan up for
reelection?"

In 1967 Ed Sullivan said, "Ingrid never forgave me for
what I had done—and she was right."

STEVE ALLEN

The so-called feud between Ed Sullivan and Steve Allen
was professional more than personal, although in the heat
of the controversy words occasionally became more bitter
than either of them would like to remember. NBC gave
Allen a variety show on Sunday nights from eight to nine
in competition with Ed Sullivan, beginning in the 1956–57
television season.

The two men were friends before the rivalry began. (Before Allen's first Sunday-night show he sent Sullivan a
wire: "Dear Ed, would you lend me ten trendex points
till payday? Love and kisses, Steve Allen.") They were
friends again after Steve Allen's program was dropped
from NBC and the goodwill continues today. In the interim
they were tough competitors. In July, 1956, Allen scored
his first rating triumph over Sullivan by booking Elvis
Presley for $7,500.

Afterward Sullivan wired Allen: "Steve Presley Allen,
NBC-TV, New York City. Stinker. Love and kisses, Ed
Sullivan." However, Sullivan countered the rating victory
by signing Presley to an exclusive contract for three appearances on his own show for $50,000. In August Steve Allen
booked Frank Sinatra and Sullivan managed to get him on
his show on the same night. In October a tribute to James

Dean was announced first for Allen's show and then for Sullivan's, provoking charges and countercharges of piracy, fibbing and sniveling. Dean ended up being memorialized on both programs.

After Sullivan failed to present Ingrid Bergman, Allen stepped in and improved his ratings with a special Bergman interview when she returned to the United States in January. On March 18, 1957, the battle for Sunday night at eight received national attention when it became the subject of a *Newsweek* cover story. "The Mugger vs. The Great Stone Face: Which one in the long run?"

In June the rivalry exploded again when Jules Green, Steve Allen's manager, said that Sullivan "unduly exploited" singer Harry Belafonte by announcing his appearance and then failing to present him. NBC questioned Sullivan's "editorial accuracy." Sullivan's comment: "I'm not getting upset about this. I've got one ulcer and I'd rather play golf than be issuing statements."

Today Sullivan remembers those days and wistfully says, "The feud was just something engineered by the NBC press department."

WALTER WINCHELL

Bitterness between Ed Sullivan and Walter Winchell began in the 1920's when Sullivan joined the Evening *Graphic* in the sports department and Winchell was the Broadway columnist. In 1928 the managing editor of the paper treated Winchell in almost sadistic fashion and Sullivan appealed to a vice-president of the paper. The editor found out and vented his fury at Sullivan, who was bitter when he was told that the informer had been Winchell himself. When Sullivan took over the Broadway column at the

Graphic, Winchell interpreted the newcomer's initial blast at Broadway columnists as a personal attack and he also felt Sullivan was copying his three-dot style of reporting.

Later Sullivan wrote an open letter to Barbara Hutton in his column in the *News* suggesting that she sponsor a Christmas party for some of the underprivileged children of New York. The heiress sent a check for $5,000 and Winchell devoted his next two columns to characterizing Sullivan as "a blackmailer." This increased the bitterness.

Later they clashed again over Josephine Baker and Sullivan blasted Winchell on Barry Gray's WMCA radio show.

In 1953 Sullivan wrote a column criticizing the Los Angeles lodge of the Friars Club which gave Winchell a dinner and allowed him to blast "other New York newspapermen."

In 1956 the feud erupted into headlines which took up the entire front page of at least one New York newspaper. At the time Winchell was just starting an NBC television series on Friday nights and he stated in a *Look* magazine article that Sullivan had kept him off CBS. Winchell said that one day he had received a phone call from Frank Stanton. "Frank asked to see me and when we met I said, 'Frank. I turned you down to stay with ABC seven years ago. Now here's your chance to turn me down. Would you consider me for things other than commentating—panels, quizzes, variety? I don't want to be off TV.'

"The answer was familiar: 'Don't worry about a thing.'

"I never heard from Frank after that. I subsequently heard that when Sullivan learned about the talk he threw a tantrum. I guess Frank decided to leave well enough alone."

When Sullivan heard about the article he told a reporter:

"This is the damnedest thing I've ever heard. It's berserk. Winchell, to rationalize his rejection by CBS, has to blame somebody. Actually I never heard of any suggestion that CBS was trying to negotiate with Winchell—it was the other way around. In any case I'm quite sure that CBS has never called upon performers for advice on who to put on TV or who to keep off. For many nauseous years this character has characterized himself as the most important guy in the country outside of the White House. Now I've become so important that I can keep him off TV."

Next it was Winchell's turn: "Sullivan's an ingrate."

Sullivan's response: "Maybe Winchell thinks a controversy will step up his ratings."

Winchell said, "I got Sullivan his first radio show and he got his first newspaper column by the grace of me being born; he got it when I switched from the old *Graphic*."

Sullivan said, "Look, I was a by-line writer for the Evening *Mail* back in 1920. That's eight or nine years before Winchell came out of the *Vaudeville News*. The guy that got me my first radio show was George M. Cohan. All I can say about Winchell is that he's real gone, gone."

Winchell said, "Sullivan would like to hitch himself to Winchell again. I've been carrying him for thirty years."

Sullivan said, "Who started this? He's the one that gave *Look* magazine the statement that I kept him off CBS. He started it."

The press asked Winchell what he thought of Steve Allen, who at that time was Sullivan's competitor. Winchell said, "I think Steve Allen's just great. Allen is just the opposite of what Fred Allen meant when he said, 'Amateurs have taken over TV. Ed Sullivan's working and Ethel Barrymore is laid off.' "

Reporters asked Sullivan what he thought of Winchell's television show, and Sullivan responded wryly that he saw the first one and "it's unfair to judge from that. You're bound to be nervous and no matter how much rehearsing you do, some things just won't come off the way they're planned."

Winchell said, "Give me a few weeks—three or four to get this show running. Then anyone who wanted to take me on, I'd be ready. Sullivan had never taken me on unless I was involved in four or five things. Then he steps in to administer the coup de groin."

"He's been traveling with that French crowd again," Sullivan retorted.

This was in 1956 when the men were evenly matched as two influential American journalists. Today the balance has changed and that, along with time, has erased the bitterness. They are friends now and have spent evenings together at the same table at El Morocco. Says Sullivan: "Winchell is the best columnist of his kind who ever lived."

JACKIE MASON

On October 18, 1964, Jackie Mason was a guest on "The Ed Sullivan Show." Midway through the broadcast the program was interrupted for a personal message from President Lyndon B. Johnson which was broadcast live over the entire network. The Sullivan show went ahead with its performance on the stage of Studio 50 and continued broadcasting live to Canada.

At 8:52, when President Johnson's speech was over, the network returned to the Sullivan show and Jackie Mason, who was finishing up his comedy routine. Mason may not have realized the show stayed on the air in Canada or that he was back on American television. However, he would probably agree that this shouldn't have influenced his behavior toward the studio audience.

At the appropriate time a staff member of the show walked behind the camera and gave Mason the usual finger signal to let him know how much time he had left. The audience had not been laughing at the routine, which seemed to unnerve the comic. He looked at the signal and then said to the audience, "Everybody's giving me the finger around here. So here's a finger for you and a finger for you and a finger for you," pointing first to the staff member behind the camera, second to Ed Sullivan and third to the studio audience. The final gesture toward the audience was an upward thrust of the third finger of the right hand, not normally seen in polite circles.

"What was visible to millions of viewers was an upward thrust of a finger by the comedian," Val Adams said in his *New York Times* television column the following day. "Mr. Mason also thumbed his nose at the camera."

After the show there was an unpleasant conversation between the two men in Sullivan's dressing room. Sullivan was outraged and felt his audience had been insulted and abused. Mason was bewildered. After Jackie left the dressing room, Sullivan wired the newspapers and the comic's manager, Bob Chartoff, to state that he was firing Mason. He was not going to pay for that evening's performance or any of the other contracted appearances of the season because Mason committed "gross insubordination," engaged in "offensive conduct" and made "obscene gestures."

Mason later filed a three-million-dollar libel and slander suit charging Sullivan with "maliciously and wickedly con-

triving to injure, blacken and defame his character, repu-
tation, profession and calling." He said that during the
dressing-room conversation Sullivan called him "a variety
of four, ten and eleven letter words of Anglo-Saxon origin
dealing generally with the subject of sex and perversion,"
and said Mason "should be run out of the entertainment
business.... I'll destroy you in show business. I'll hurt
you in every way I can.... You did dirty things on my
program."

In September, 1966, Sullivan and Mason made up. "Sylvia and I were at the Las Vegas airport when I saw a
familiar face. I said Hello and reached out to shake the
man's hand when I realized it was Jackie Mason. Well, I
don't carry grudges. I told him that I was willing to let
bygones be bygones, and right there I invited him back on
the show—and he appeared shortly thereafter."

On the night of Mason's return the comic was confused
by the lack of press interest in the reunion. He couldn't
understand why reporters weren't hanging around and
phoning as they had done two years before. He turned
to the older and wiser showman for an explanation. The
answer was, "Don't you know, Jackie, that when people
fight, that's news. There's no story when they make up."

AND OTHERS

In 1960 Sullivan was scheduled to present a film of Barry
Fitzgerald interviewing Sean O'Casey on his St. Patrick's
Day program. There were many protests from people who
consider O'Casey anticlerical ("all literate") and Sullivan
decided not to show the segment. This brought new ob-
jections from the pro-O'Casey crowd and now Sullivan

couldn't win. In the end he did not present the sequence. "The show was a friendly gesture to the Irish for St. Patrick's Day, so I decided to cancel the film." On air he said, "I had planned to use some film on Sean O'Casey but I got so many calls, nice phone calls, asking to delete that and in respect to their wishes I have deleted it."

One of the severest critics of Sullivan's action was Brooks Atkinson, then drama critic of *The New York Times*. Sullivan tried to explain in a letter:

> Dear Mr. Atkinson,
>
> My eagerness to present Sean O'Casey was indicated by the fact that I scheduled him. I sent out wires to the New York dramatic critics inviting them to see this, the first time I've ever done this in the twelve-year history of our show. However, the flood of protesting telephone calls to our studio during the afternoon attacking Sean as an ideological symbol, persuaded me to delete it. Allegedly O'Casey, in England, has permitted himself to be used by the communists and it was on this ground that I based my decision. I found myself in the indefensible position of recently asking the country and Canada to save 150 Hungarian youngsters from the Hungarian communists' noose and then, a few months later, presenting a literary giant who apparently had failed to speak out against this and other outrages.
>
> Sincerely,

Atkinson was not persuaded and did not forget. The following month *Bye Bye Birdie* opened on Broadway and the critic's review described how a teen-age idol gave one last kiss on the Sullivan show in a segment "no doubt replacing the Sean O'Casey interview."

In May, 1963, folksinger Bob Dylan was off the show at the last minute when CBS said his song "The Talking John

Birch Society Blues" was "controversial." Said *The New York Times:* "The network's stand was opposed by Mr. Sullivan and by Bob Precht, producer of the program, who had approved of the lampoon of the right-wing organization." This episode, involving the network in conflict not only with a popular folksinger but with one of its most important stars, could have been magnified in a sensational way if the people involved had not been restrained.

A scene from *The Subject Was Roses* was scheduled for the program, but author Frank D. Gilroy insisted that the guests be Jack Albertson and Irene Daley of the original cast. Sullivan wanted Chester Morris and Maureen O'Sullivan, then playing the roles on Broadway. He liked their performances and their names meant more on the marquee. The dispute was not resolved and the scene was never shown.

The F.C.C. started an investigation after a film of Fonteyn and Nureyev was announced and then canceled on two consecutive weeks in 1966. The dancers were scheduled for the October 2 program in *Romeo and Juliet,* but the show ran long and it was decided to postpone this film segment rather than a live performer. On October 9 the film was shown at the dress rehearsal, the first time it had been seen outside the screening room, and the quality was so poor it could not be aired. "Misrepresenting" the appearance of two stars for two successive weeks was the inevitable result of late changes on a live show and early newspaper deadlines for television listings. This was hard for the people writing letters of protest to understand.

Mary Tyler Moore was signed for two appearances at $7,500 a program. She spent the week in New York re-

hearsing a song-and-dance number but as Sunday approached it became clear there was a misunderstanding
between her and the program. She planned to tape the
vocal portions of her number in advance but the show
expected her to sing live and not mouth the lyrics. The
situation could not be resolved and amid bitter words and
hard feelings, all private, Mary Tyler Moore was off the
program. She went to court to collect $15,000 for the two
appearances, and if either Sullivan or Miss Moore had
been eager for publicity, here was a natural for page one.
But they wanted to handle a difficult situation discreetly
and they kept quiet about the battle. The case went to
court and Miss Moore collected $7,500 (instead of her
$15,000) and though it was a matter of public record, few
people knew what was going on. An alert reporter could
have gotten a good story for himself.

The truth about the Sid Caesar-Nancy Walker sketch
on May 2, 1965, never made the papers at all. At dress
rehearsal the two comedy stars appeared in a routine involving an automobile which did not get laughs from
the audience. Sullivan wanted to tighten it up but Caesar
was not agreeable. Finally the two men decided that the
best solution was to drop the sketch from the show even
though it was listed in the papers as one of the highlights
of the evening. Because Sid Caesar and Nancy Walker are
talented performers and nice people, Sullivan did not want
it known their sketch didn't work. He knew it could hurt
them professionally. As it happened, the sketch presented
numerous mechanical problems. It was decided to play up
that aspect if the press called and discuss the mechanical
failure of the car, not the sketch. That is what happened

and on May 4, 1965, the following story appeared on page
three of the New York *Journal-American:*

Caesar's Car Backfires on T.V.

Comic Sid Caesar is still puzzling today over how to make
the right things go wrong and the wrong things go right in an
auto comedy skit guaranteed to give members of the National Safety Council nightmares. Millions missed the comedian on CBS-TV's "Ed Sullivan Show" last night precisely
because the right things didn't go wrong in the right way.

"We were attempting to do a skit involving an automobile,
but the props just didn't work right," explained Mr. Sullivan
after the show, which subbed a tape of English singer Dusty
Springfield and an extra vocal by the Rolling Stones in Mr.
Caesar's scheduled spot.

"In the skit Sid is giving a driving lesson to his wife,
played by Nancy Walker. She gets behind the wheel and
everything is supposed to go wrong. She's supposed to shift
and the trunk is supposed to fly open. When she turns on the
windshield wipers, water is supposed to spray them.

"The hood is supposed to keep popping up. The tires are
supposed to collapse and one of the doors is supposed to fall
off. But when he tried it in dress rehearsal, everything went
wrong, that is, nothing went wrong in the right way.

"The stagehands tried to get it in working order but it became too unwieldy. It was too risky to go on the show with
it. Sid said it was too tough to attempt. He said, 'let me come
back another week.'

"What else could we do? It was mechanical failure."

Thus a Sid Caesar-Ed Sullivan feud was kept out of
print.

Other incidents, all handled quietly, were: The dropping
of a British rock-and-roll group from a Sullivan program
because the Immigration Department decided there were
"equally capable" American groups available—a touchy

episode because it could have jeopardized the program's relationship with the Labor Department; a lawsuit by Westbrook Pegler against CBS and the program after Sullivan presented Van Heflin in a scene from the Broadway play *A Case of Libel* based on Louis Nizer's version of the Pegler-Quentin Reynolds lawsuit; the "firing" of Jerry Vale and the Ramsey Lewis Trio after they violated the exclusivity clauses in their contract by making local television appearances with Mike Douglas and Murray the K, respectively; Dinah Shore off the show in a dispute over "time and material"; the sudden pre-show departure of Vince Edwards (said Sullivan: "We don't want him and anyway he's no singer.").

When Ed Sullivan is attacked, his first inclination is to strike back. When he is angry, he talks frankly. "One of these days I may learn not to open my mouth so quickly," he says. But most of the time he does stop to analyze the situation. He decides the wisest course of action unemotionally and objectively and goes out of his way to avoid a public controversy, whether it be with Mary Tyler Moore, Sid Caesar or Dinah Shore. The years have made him a more patient and understanding man, and today he is far more likely to say nothing than something bad.

His daughter Betty sums it up: "He's mellowed a lot. He used to get angry and feel deeply about things. He doesn't any more."

12

The Complex Man

Ask any two people what Ed Sullivan is like and you will get two different answers. This was illustrated when several members of his staff were requested to describe him in one sentence, using the first words that came into their minds that conveyed what he was like.

One person said: "He's an astute person, knowledgeable in world affairs." Said another: "He knows exactly what he's doing, and nobody's proved him wrong in all these years." A third said: "He's a legend in his own time." A fourth: "The show comes first and the people on it don't exist for him outside of their functions." A fifth: "He's never too busy to say hello and ask about your family." Other comments, all from people now working on the Sullivan show: "I wouldn't want to be his enemy"; "He's great to work for if he gets what he wants when he wants it"; "He's terrific. I really like him"; "He forgets things"; "He's fine if you keep him busy; when he has nothing to do he thinks up ways to make work for everyone," and "He's a nice man, kind. In fact, he is sort of like a little boy."

However, Ed Sullivan cannot be characterized by any

single quality. He is more than anything else complex and
filled with contradictions. He is friendly, aloof, playful,
sarcastic, cool, volatile, smooth and awkward. Even his
closest friends find him a difficult man to understand. One
reason is his tremendous introversion or, as he calls it,
"shyness." "I'm shy, terribly, almost painfully shy." He
keeps things to himself and seldom explains his reasons for
doing something.

On one of the rare occasions that Sylvia and Betty came
to the studio, the talent agents who were watching the show
on a television set in his dressing room did not get up and
give the women their seats. When Sullivan learned of this
later, he was furious but never said anything to the men.
He told the backstage guard that in the future no one was
allowed in the room during the show. "The agents should
be downstairs applauding the acts." None of the men ever
associated their banishment with the incident of the seats
and to them—as on other occasions—his behavior seemed
arbitrary and eccentric.

Much of the time he doesn't explain his actions even to
himself. He operates on instinct with a great intuitive sense
of what is right for him. He feels it is inappropriate to pose
for undignified pictures that make him look ridiculous and
refuses to do so. Yet he agreed to be photographed in a
Beatle wig for an *Esquire* cover because his instincts told
him that was an exception and would be all right.

He is sensitive and easily hurt. "I want people to like
me. If I'm out for dinner and get a cold stare, it can wreck
the evening for me."

A cruel remark from a stranger can hit him hard. A man
came up to him at the prizefights and said, "I saw your show
last Sunday. It really stunk."

"I'm sorry to hear that," Sullivan replied and walked away. He tried to shake off the insult and said to his friends, "There are nuts like that all over the place," but the hurt stayed with him for a long while that night.

He is most comfortable in small groups of people he knows well. "I dread big affairs of any kind. I can go out with close friends and not feel shy at all, but if there's one person in the group I don't know, if I feel someone is just a little bit hostile, I clam up. It's a terrible feeling."

Trivial and unimportant things can upset him enormously. He knows this about himself. "Big problems seldom faze me but little things annoy me a great deal. I get very irate, for instance, when agents try to outsmart me on a deal after they have signed for an artist's appearance on the show. I just can't take pettiness."

When something bothers him, his mood can shift suddenly from openness to withdrawal. He was friendly to a reporter who was questioning him on the show. The man asked why he didn't present scenes from operas lavishly and Sullivan said he learned in 1956 after his "Toast to the Met" that the numbers only worked when the stars wore evening clothes and not costumes. Then the reporter wanted to know why he was successful when he broke the old show-business rule and put two comedy acts back to back. Sullivan answered, "You can do it if they are different kinds of comedy." Then he thought about the questions and the reporter's overly eager manner and decided the man was prying. He closed up tight and was unresponsive for the remainder of the interview. Later he said privately, "I'm not going to give away all my secrets."

One night he spent an enjoyable social evening with a popular singer and there was no business talk. At the end of the night the singer asked Sullivan to put him on the show to push his new record. It was taking unfair advantage of a social situation. Sullivan answered that he would introduce him from the audience. "When you do, will you mention the record?" Sullivan's face tightened. He remained superficially pleasant, but the genuine friendliness was gone. He ended up introducing the singer, but he never plugged the record.

The change in Sullivan's moods baffles people who know him as well as those who don't. He can get tremendously excited about a performer and cool off, be friendly one day and icy the next, but he will probably never say why. The shift in attitude will go unexplained, just as the agents never found out the reason they couldn't watch the show in his dressing room.

Sullivan is adept at hiding his true feelings behind a mask and perceiving more than he reveals. On one occasion he described his "stone face" as a defense against shyness. "I once did my show playing a clown. I loved it. Behind makeup I could always be myself, but without it I often feel I am just a baggy-eyed old man."

For all his restraint, the unpredictable Ed Sullivan will sometimes let himself go in remarkable ways. He was very emotional the evening he arrived at a friend's house to find there was a surprise sixty-fifth birthday party and the afternoon he was told by CBS that the name of Studio 50 was being changed to The Ed Sullivan Theater. On both occasions he cried.

"People think he's cold. It's only a front. There's an exceptionally warm man underneath," says Ray Bloch. Betty Precht puts it another way: "He's a nice human being. If you can leave that impression behind, you've accomplished something." Sullivan himself values warmth in others: "If people aren't kind, they're nothing. The rest comes out of a machine."

One weekend a young boy from Providence, Rhode Island, came to New York with a local disc jockey and stayed with his grandmother. The parents thought he was too young for the trip but the grandmother persuaded them it would be a good experience. He was put in the disc jockey's care and they spent Sunday at the studio where they talked with a popular rock-and-roll group. When the youngster walked out of the stage door, some teen-age girls reached out to touch him because they either mistook him for a singer or realized he had just met the group. The boy became scared and ran. The girls chased after him and he leaped into the street to get away. An automobile rounded the corner and he was struck and killed. Sullivan had never met the youngster, but when he heard what had happened he contacted the family right away. The grief-stricken parents and the grandmother were almost beyond consolation, but Sullivan met with them and tried to make them not blame themselves. Nobody ever knew about it but the family.

Another episode makes a quaint Christmas story. Years before the Sullivan show a Broadway press agent was about to lose some restaurants and nightclubs as clients and needed the money. Sullivan heard about it on Christmas Eve and accompanied the man to his clubs that night so the owners would know the press agent was in solid with columnist Sullivan. He saved the accounts but got home late for his own family celebration.

One of Ed's closest friends was Bill "Bojangles" Robinson (after whom he named his poodle), and in November,

1949, Robinson died, penniless. Sullivan raised money for
the funeral from a number of sources, including his own
wallet. He made the arrangements with Carmine's help
and they were spectacular in Sullivan's best style. All of
the flags on Broadway were flown at half-mast. Police estimated that half a million people lined the streets and
rooftops to view the motorcade from Harlem's Abyssinian
Baptist Church to Evergreen Cemetery in Brooklyn. There
were three thousand people inside the church and a hundred
thousand people listening to the services over loudspeakers
outside. Adam Clayton Powell delivered the sermon. "Bill
had only two sins, ice cream and gambling," he said. The
people inside the church chuckled and a moment later a
second chuckle was heard from the larger crowd in the streets.

Sullivan lined up an all-star cast including Danny Kaye,
Milton Berle, Jimmy Durante, Arthur Treacher, Ethel
Merman, Rochester, Jackie Robinson, Sugar Ray Robinson,
Louis Armstrong, W. C. Handy, Hazel Scott and Mrs. Irv-
ing Berlin. As the star-studded funeral procession passed
through Harlem, there was "a complete and reverent hush."
Not one of the tens of thousands of neighborhood school-
children rushed up for autographs.

For all his warmth Ed Sullivan is a fighter and will battle
hard for what he believes. As a profiler noted, "He has
survived in the jungle. No one survives in the jungle on
kindness alone." He is a determined man and, if challenged,
will go out of his way to prove that he's right.

In 1962 he was advised against devoting an entire show
to the Piccoli Puppets. He was told this one act could not
carry a whole show. He went ahead anyway, and to prove
to his associates that he was right in his decision, he asked
his audience to write letters telling him how they liked the

show. He received "an estimated 120,000 letters and cards." He underscored his point by bringing the mailbags out on his stage live from New York.

The week after he returned from Expo 67 he gave an enthusiastic endorsement of the fair at his dress rehearsal. The CBS "censor" told him this kind of plug was against company policy. Sullivan politely agreed. On air that night he did not say he liked Expo 67. He said that all his reporter friends told him to go to the fair because it was the most wonderful fair in the history of expositions. If CBS insisted on rules, fine. He was following this one to the letter. But no one was going to push Ed Sullivan around.

His manner can be forbidding and many people are afraid of him. When the Russian ballerina Maya Plisetskaya was on the program, he called her Maria at dress rehearsal. Some members of his staff caught the error but were scared to tell him, and when he introduced the dancer on air, it was still Maria.

The ominous exterior hints at the tremendous anger that can come to the surface when he feels someone has taken advantage of him. When Dick Haymes was married to Fran Jeffries, they were scheduled to perform together on the program. Haymes got sick at the last minute and was having trouble getting hold of a doctor. Sullivan sent his own. On the night of the show he presented Fran Jeffries as a solo performer and paid the couple the full amount they would have received if both of them had performed. There was an understanding that when Haymes was well again, they would make their first joint appearance on the Sullivan show. Later the host heard they signed to be guests on another variety program before his, and his reaction toward their ingratitude was unprintable. He saw to it that

their first booking as a couple was on the Sullivan show. He
didn't ask them back a second time.

His makeup man was given an assignment to go to New
Jersey where Sullivan was appearing on a local television
show. Since it was not a CBS station, the man presumed he
would be paid by Sullivan and not the network, which at
that time picked up his tab. Afterward he called the producer's office asking for his check and presumed it would
be mailed shortly. Someone on the show told Sullivan but
did not relay all the facts. The host was furious that after
an association of many years the man was unwilling to do a
small favor without pay. Without speaking to him first,
Sullivan fired him from the show (though not CBS). When
the makeup man wrote Sullivan a letter of explanation, he
was reinstated.

One Sunday before Christmas in 1966 Sullivan asked his
orchestra to play "Silent Night," but the musicians' union
wanted an additional $900 because the song was not part of
the regular show. Sullivan was furious and yelled at the
musicians' representative for fifteen minutes. He cited the
large sums of money the program had paid into the union
coffers over the years and said that if the union rule couldn't
be waived, he didn't have to employ nineteen musicians
every week. His contract required a minimum of eight, and
the other eleven men shouldn't bother showing up the following week because they were fired. He was still in a rage
when he walked away and the musicians' representative was
trembling. During the week the dispute was settled amica-
bly. There were nineteen musicians on the show the following week and Sullivan didn't pay $900 for "Silent Night."

Executives at his own company know from their own
experience that he is a tough man to tangle with. When he

wants something, he fights until he gets it. He asked for color at a time it was difficult to provide, and CBS told him it wasn't possible then. He "persuaded" them that it was.

Sometimes he expresses his anger in oblique ways. One Sunday he was introducing Paul Gallico from the audience, and before air time a network representative checking out the program content asked the host who Gallico was. Sullivan was annoyed that the man was not familiar with such a well-known writer and also felt his own editorial judgment was being questioned. "Gallico is a struggling young author, and I'm going to help him out with a little publicity," the host said with an icy sarcasm so subtle that the man mistook it for a friendly, serious response. The next day Sullivan telephoned a CBS vice-president to complain about the incident and said he would not sign his CBS contract, then up for renewal, unless that kind of harassment stopped.

Sullivan is just as aroused when the person being taken advantage of is someone other than himself. A visitor to his apartment tripped over a carpet that was improperly placed in the lobby, pointed it out to a bellboy, and instead of receiving an apology was told not to be so clumsy. When Sullivan heard about it, he went downstairs to complain. He asked his guest to identify the bellboy, but the man pretended to forget, knowing Sullivan would want the employee fired on the spot.

Once he heard that a network man assigned to his show had been unfairly criticized by his boss. Sullivan telephoned the boss and threatened to have him fired if the incident reoccurred.

Nothing arouses the fighter in him more than prejudice. He was a crusader for the Negro long before it became fashionable and overcame a great deal of opposition to present an integrated show. He was the first television host to do so. There was never any question in his mind about using Negroes on television, although in the early years there was plenty of question on the part of television.

When Emerson Radio became the first sponsor in 1948, the company assembled their salesmen from all over the country in New York for a luncheon to meet Sullivan and mark the signing of the contract. Southern salesmen argued he should drop Negro stars. "It will ruin business," they said. He told them that he didn't believe it. "Time was to demonstrate that they were wrong, because our show year after year has been top rated in the deep South and still is. It would be impossible to put on a worthwhile show without availing one's self of Negro talent. You couldn't stay on top all these years as we have without having southerners look at your show. If the time ever came when I couldn't exercise complete freedom on the talent I'd selected, I'd get the hell off. In booking acts I've never thought in terms of religion or color and I've brought in acts from all over the world. I'm looking solely for fine performers who have something on the ball."

Later, dealers and advertising agencies continued trying to persuade him not to use Negro entertainers. His answer: "They're going on the show. If you want to get the hell out, fine."

In May, 1951, Ed Sullivan wrote an article in *Ebony* magazine entitled, "Can TV Crack America's Color Line?" In recounting Negro performers who had been on his program during the first three years, he said:

> In every way television seems to have a special niche for the Negro. As one of the pioneers in television, I am proud that I've had the very real opportunity to present so many

Negro performers to so great an audience. But as I have come to realize down the years, we need to do nothing special for the Negro in television or in any other phase of American life. As I see it, the Negro neither wants nor needs special consideration but only the decent and full opportunity every other American merits and should enjoy.

In 1950 Sullivan received a letter that he said illustrated this point. It was from a viewer who wrote: "Probably I am much more liberal in viewpoint than you, but I wish to ask a question. When you have Negro stars on the show, it seems to me that you always make a point of shaking hands with them. This is as it should be, but tell me one thing: Why don't you shake hands with your white performers?" The letter was perceptive, and from then on he was shaking hands with white stars too.

One might think that an event as important as the permanent integration of a television chorus line for the first time would have been carefully planned. It happened on the Sullivan show in a way which also illustrates the star's public-relations skill and shows the instinctive way he operates.

On December 3, 1961, he presented the All-America football team and had eleven girls dancing with the players during their introductions. There was one Negro athlete, Bobby Bell, and the show hired one Negro dancer, Myrna White, to be his partner. On December 5 *Jet* magazine called Sullivan to say hundreds of letters and phone calls had come in about this segment, and 80 percent of them were critical. *Jet* wanted an explanation and planned to do a controversial cover story on the incident. Sullivan turned a difficult public-relations situation into a triumph by refusing to be defensive.

Sullivan said to *Jet:* "What's wrong with having Myrna White dance with Bobby Bell? Bell is a fine young man, two-time All-American, and any girl would be proud to dance with him. Would you object if your sister danced with Bobby Bell? Let's work together on this. Cut out the sniping. Our show has done more to help Negroes than any other on television. Don't louse it up."

While he was talking he decided to have Myrna White back on the show the following week and make her a permanent member of the chorus line. On the spur of the moment he suggested a new angle for the cover story. Write about the first permanent Negro chorus girl on television, he said. And they did.

There was a follow-up story in the April *Ebony* magazine that included a picture layout of Myrna White. The title of the article was "Myrna White Scores Dance Success," and underneath in slightly smaller type "Broadway Dancer Integrates Chorus Line on Ed Sullivan Television Show." The article began: "When nimble Myrna White twisted with Minnesota's All-American football star Bobby Bell on the Ed Sullivan TV show in December, it marked the first time the program had integrated a Negro in its permanent dance troupe...."

It is Sullivan's interest not just in the Negro but in all minority groups that has contributed to the program's continuing popularity. At every opportunity he mentions a hometown, a nationality, or the name of an organization, and all of the many small groups combine to make an influential majority. His penchant for this kind of classification was treated dryly by *The New Yorker* magazine in 1958. They printed the following Sullivan quotation:

"Americans of Italian blood are getting a great wallop

out of Nashua, Kentucky Derby favorite, as his great granddaddy was the Italian horse Nearco, sire of Nasrullah.
The Derby will be an all-paisan affair with Arcaro aboard
Nashua." The magazine's comment: "You'll probably recall that Americans of Italian blood expressed the great
wallop they got from this state of affairs in scenes of wild
excitement from coast to coast as soon as they had it straight
in their minds whether it was Arcaro who was Nashua's
granddaddy, with Nearco aboard, or vice versa."

Ed Sullivan's life revolves around the program. He thinks
about it all the time, and there is no such thing for him as
outside interests—only sports and entertainment. Today he
is less intense than in the past, but no matter where he is,
he never gets so absorbed in what he is doing that he completely forgets about his job. He will go to Yonkers to relax
at the trotting races and one of the jockeys will end up on
the show. During his summer vacation, when the program is
already on tape, he will go into the studio at the last minute
and add a timely insert.

His preoccupation with the show is one of the reasons he
sometimes appears nervous and ill at ease on camera. He is
simply tense and keyed up and apprehensive that something
will go wrong. He once said that he looked uncomfortable
because his mind was on so many things between eight and
nine, from the stagehands making too much noise backstage
to the comedians not getting enough laughs out front.

"Well, of course the show is my whole life, outside of my
family, of course. What else is there? I enjoy it, I love television, and I love to work. I'll never retire. What would I
do if I didn't have this show? I'm so darn lucky because
I've had a ringside seat and have gotten to know some
of the greatest figures in show business. I'm working or

thinking about it all the time. I would say I've given it about as much as I can. They took out my ulcer, then they took out my gall bladder. I haven't got much else to give it."

There is no area of the program in which he has not been involved at one time or another, from the music to the costumes. When the network writes about the show, he will correct the spelling, grammar, punctuation and paragraphing of the rough draft as if he were the copy editor. When something comes to his attention, he cannot stay on the sidelines but takes over. If he gives the responsibility to someone else he will not relax until he has checked and double checked to make certain his wishes are carried out. He will have three different people relay instructions to a fourth, and then when he sees the fourth man himself he will repeat everything again.

"Ed likes to do everything himself. He doesn't want help," Sylvia says.

He will rely on his staff for little things, but deep down he knows that he is responsible for his own success and if necessary he could do it alone all over again. In twenty years no one in his professional life has been indispensable or essential to his success.

Because he is a one-man operation he has never built an organization or produced anything besides his own program. As a pioneer in the medium he was in a position to create a successful independent production company and present other television programs. Popular performers who followed him, like Lucille Ball, Desi Arnaz and Danny Thomas, did just that and founded their own business empires. Sullivan did not because he isn't an administrator and cannot delegate authority. He observes the difference in this respect between himself and his producer Bob Precht, who has also

produced other shows under the Sullivan Productions name.
"If I were over in his office, I wouldn't be able to let everyone do his own separate job the way Bob does. I'd start
trying to do it all myself. He can assign jobs. I'd assign them
and get into them too. I just can't delegate authority
that way."

It is Ed Sullivan's show in more than name. He once said
jokingly, "If it takes punch to get my own way when I'm
convinced I'm right, I think I can out punch the rest of
them." He has the final say on everything and will not tol-
erate interference from advertising agencies, stars, sponsors
or talent agents. As head man he goes to no one for approval.
"Other shows aren't that fortunate," he says. Beatles' manager Brian Epstein said to him once, "I would like to know
the exact wording of your introduction." Sullivan replied
coolly, "I would like you to get lost."

Ed Sullivan operates best under pressure. He never panics
but remains incredibly cool and handles difficult situations
adeptly. When the show is traveling and there are moments
of unusual strain that make other people tense and irritable,
he will be relaxed and a model of calmness.

He knows his own strengths and weaknesses and has a remarkable knack for looking at himself objectively. A reporter for a national magazine told Sullivan he was having
trouble putting together a well-rounded article because
nobody had anything bad to say about him. The host went
home, compiled a list of people who would make critical
statements and starred the ones who would also be witty.
He was so capable of viewing himself dispassionately that
he identified with the reporter. The story ended up as a
highly flattering piece without a critical remark. Perhaps

Sullivan's instincts told him that in advance and providing
the list may have insured a complimentary article.

Another writer in whom he had a personal interest said
he was putting together a "valentine" and Sullivan replied,
"You'd better write about my temper too. Valentines don't
sell."

He has a clear picture of the image he wants for himself,
and arrogance is not part of it. Viewers know that he speaks
in superlatives and nothing is ever big or great but "really
big" and "all-time great." "The most exciting act we've
presented in all of our twenty years" applies to hundreds
of performers and generally someone on a very recent
show. But he avoids immodest descriptions of himself. "I'm
the best damn showman on television" has been reprinted
often, but it was taken out of context from a *New York
Times* article of ten years ago. It is an uncharacteristic
phrase that he would not use. In many ways he still sees
himself as the boy from Port Chester instead of in exalted
terms.

This modest self-appraisal also shows up in a lack of
vanity. He dyes his hair but with reluctance. The bags
under his eyes don't bother him but he has been told they
look terrible on television. He was persuaded to enter the
hospital in June, 1967, to have them removed by cosmetic
surgery. After he was in his room a few hours, he got dressed,
went for a walk and never returned. He just wasn't interested in that kind of operation.

When he can, he will edit a piece of copy to conform to
his self-image, as if he were writing about a third person,
not himself. "Ed Sullivan is probably the single most powerful and influential performer in all of television. One reason
is his longevity, which gives him the advantage of valuable

contacts" was rewritten by him to read: "Ed Sullivan, whose TV show is now in its twentieth continuous year and still top rated, has a track record in TV which gives him the advantage of valuable contacts." He rejected the designation of "single most powerful and influential."

He is a realist and when he cannot make changes, he will accept the inevitable with good grace. If he is confronted by an accomplished fact, such as an article that is already in print, he will judge it for what it is and not for what it might have been. He accepts reality in the truest meaning of the phrase, and this ability to adjust to changing situations is an important factor in his success.

Ed Sullivan is a creature of habit who is likely to do something the same way indefinitely after he does it twice. He eats in the same restaurants all the time. When he started taking pictures with friends after the show, it was a certainty he would continue. He brought an instrumental group from the Delmonico to warm up the audience before the program, and it was inevitable they would return weekly.

But, like President Johnson, he dislikes being taken for granted and is determined to be unpredictable. He is capable of breaking a habit of long standing without warning. One Sunday the Delmonico musicians were not there. It was obvious then that their absence would become a habit and they would never be back again. Instead, audio tapes were substituted (and more recently live musicians from a night spot, Your Father's Mustache). Every Christmas he showcased the Friendship Tree, a promotion to attach Christmas cards to trees for hospitals, which was sponsored by a major tape concern. One year the firm's public-relations man irritated him and suddenly that was the end of it.

He feels comfortable having familiar faces around the studio and most of the people on the program have had their jobs for years. However, he is flexible enough to adapt to a whole new set of faces if that should be necessary.

For all his intensity, there is still time for humor. At the height of his feud with Steve Allen, one of Allen's writers, Herb Sargent, decided to give his boss an unusual Christmas present. Sargent went to Sullivan, whom he had never met before, and asked if he would pose for a picture showing Sargent and another of Allen's writers giving Sullivan material and Sullivan giving them money in return. Sullivan agreed. He liked the gag.

On another occasion he was to meet a staff member at Madison Square Garden to pose for still pictures with circus performers. His man arrived on time but there was no sign of Sullivan, only a clown and a Ringling representative, who was complaining about the host's tardiness. The clown nodded his head in agreement and playfully shoved his face in front of the new arrival several times. Finally the clown spoke for the first time. "When did you say Sullivan was coming?" he asked. The voice was Sullivan's. He had arrived early and successfully tested his makeup.

When Tammy Grimes was on the show, she told him she lived on Bank Street and Sullivan said that was where he used to live. He added, kiddingly, "Let me know if you come across one of my old socks." A few weeks later Sullivan received one dirty sock in the mail without a note. He had forgotten the conversation and figured that the pro at the Westchester Country Club was forwarding an article of clothing he had left. It wasn't until several months later, when Tammy Grimes returned to the show, that he found out the truth. She asked him if he had received his sock, and he did a fantastic double take and collapsed in laughter.

Very often he is the object of the laughter, and this is usually because of his incredible forgetfulness. Once he was in Las Vegas with one of his staff and extended a casual dinner invitation on three or four different occasions over a three-day period, forgetting each time that he had done so before. On the plane back he said, "Why don't we have dinner one of these days?"

He met someone in Miami who inquired about a man on his staff. "Terrifically nice guy, but he's not with us anymore. He's on a daytime soap or something," Sullivan said. The man replied that he had seen this fellow's name on the credits the Sunday before but Sullivan insisted he was mistaken. When the staff man heard about the episode, he decided to show his face more often at the studio.

Sullivan had an appointment in the new CBS headquarters building, where he had never been before, and was instructed to go to the southeast corner of 53rd Street and Sixth Avenue. He went to the building on the northeast corner and asked for the CBS executive. The receptionist in the lobby recognized him and sent him across the street. He was in the ABC building.

He told his studio audience at the Expo theater in Montreal to write to the CBS ticket office if they were coming to New York and wanted to see the show over the summer, forgetting that he had decided not to present live programs during those months but shows already on tape.

On another occasion he asked someone on his staff to check out a new group called "The Young Rascals," which he heard had a big record. "But Mr. Sullivan," was the reply, "The Young Rascals were on our show last Sunday."

When Sullivan greeted one of his men by name backstage, someone else on the show remarked afterward, "He must really like you. You've only worked for him for five years and he remembers your name already." Another listener added, "When he knows your name, you're in trouble." (Though he may forget the name of his costume designer or lighting man, he is just as likely to recall the stagehand's.)

On one occasion a reporter asked him who his closest friends were. He mentioned four or five people and then said, "And of course Ben Sokolow's wife. Now what is her name? Darn it, I just can't think of it for the moment." On the same occasion he was asked his age and turned to an associate for the answer.

When Sullivan's mistakes hold him up to ridicule, he can be hurt or angry. But sometimes he will be the first to laugh at himself, as he did when he introduced Dolores Gray from the audience as "starving on Broadway in *Sherry*." He was so amused that he rebroadcast the segment the following week. It all depends on how something is said. When a reporter called his show "nothing but vaudeville" he explained in detail why it wasn't. Another writer said Sullivan presented "the best vaudeville of the twentieth century" and then he didn't mind the word.

People meeting him for the first time expect an awkward and inarticulate man because of his television personality and are surprised to find that he is poised and completely in command of the situation. No one in the world can be more charming when he is in the mood. He establishes a rapport quickly and comes across as warm, friendly, casual, easygoing, good-natured—the epitome of "the regular guy." His tone of voice is equally pleasant whether he is talking to a plumber or a head of state.

He is enormously gracious and courtly in an old-world way. He never closes the door on a departing visitor but waits in the hall until the elevator arrives. He stands up when a lady comes to the table and always lights her cigarette. When the Sullivans take a woman friend of theirs back to her home in the Ritz Tower, there is a doorman out front. Sullivan could wait in the car and be certain she got inside safely, but he always walks her to the door. He extends the same graciousness to everyone in his party. If he is having dinner with a celebrity and a stranger asks for his autograph but does not recognize the other person, he is likely to say to his friend, "Jerry, why don't you sign first." The agents who didn't give the ladies their seats in his dressing room especially irritated him because he expects other people's manners to be like his own. He has a chivalrous attitude toward women, and it is not unlike the Walter Scott books of his youth.

A reporter will get a cordial welcome to Suite 1102. Sullivan is an outgoing host with a knack for making a guest feel at home. He will come to the door dressed casually in a sport shirt and slacks, invite the visitor into the living room and offer a seat on the couch while he sits on a chair. "How are you? Nice to see you," he will say, and sound like he is talking to a valued friend. He has developed the habit of calling men "How are you" or "Hi there" and women "honey" to protect himself from his bad memory for names, and he does it without sounding affected. The habit carries over to strangers whom he would not be expected to know.

His favorite hour for interviews is twelve thirty and, since there is never any food in the house except a jar of sour balls on the coffee table, this is apt to play havoc with the visitor's appetite.

Sullivan responds to questions in a sort of free-association way. A query about mental health may produce a story about Josh Logan, which will remind him of Helen Hayes and Robert E. Sherwood, and he will wind up his answer talking about the Beatles.

He is meticulous about small details and will buzz Carmine on the interoffice phone for the information. "Carmine, when did we have the Moiseyev Dancers on our show?" or "How much did we pay the Beatles?" If Carmine is away and Sylvia is in the next room, he will call on her memory to verify a fact. When he relates an anecdote, he carefully spells out the proper names like a newsman phoning in a story to the city desk. He tries to answer every question, no matter how remote it is from his own experience. When a reporter asked how a young fellow starts off at the *News*, he picked up the phone, dialed the paper, asked for personnel, identified himself, and got the answer.

He has never terminated an interview by himself. He waits for the reporter to say he must go or for a third person to find a gracious way of ending it.

Sullivan particularly enjoys being with sports celebrities and has always been star-struck by them. "I like people . . . all people, but especially athletes and performers." In his dressing room before a show, his feelings are particularly obvious as he glows with admiration while chatting with a star athlete he is going to introduce from the audience.

"Basically I'm a sportswriter and my show shows it. Throughout the years I've had the greats in sports on my show. On those occasions I felt very much at home." He thinks of himself as a sports reporter and still takes pride in his sporting scoops which included disclosing that Bobby Jones was quitting amateur golf to make golf movie shorts and witnessing Jack Dempsey refuse to give $50,000 in Chicago to fix a referee for the second Tunney fight.

His afternoons used to be filled with golf, though he doesn't play anymore. His partners have included such diverse personalities as the Duke of Windsor, Henry Ford and Vice President Nixon.

Buddy Hackett called him "the most gentlemanly golfer I ever played with." Peter Lind Hayes said he was "the only golfer who falls asleep on his own backswing," and Bob Hope also joked about the slowness. Once he said, "Hit it quick before your clothes go out of style." Reporter Hal Humphrey wrote:

> Ed has a way of addressing a golf ball which causes those playing with him to wonder what they had been doing wrong. As he bends over the ball, Ed shakes his head three or four times as if in disbelief that anything that small could be hit. On the fourth shake he kind of shrugs both shoulders as if saying to himself, "oh-come-on-what-the-hell, I'll give it a try," then smacks it right down the middle of the fairway. He sinks ten and fifteen foot putts with that same head-shaking move.

The 1942–43 season was his best and he averaged between seventy and seventy-two strokes a round. He was called "the most over-proed golfer in the country" because so many of the top golfing stars are his friends and gave him advice. On one occasion eight different pros instructed him simultaneously, one pro assigned to his left foot, a second focusing on his hip action, another on his shoulder turn, and so on.

Ed Sullivan likes enthusiastic people ". . . outgoing people like Sylvia," especially if they are relaxed, low-keyed, not tense.

Most of all Sullivan likes the professional. "I'm in ab-
solute awe of people who do things well." His wife says,
"If he sees a street cleaner who is really polishing the pave-
ment, he'll say, 'Look at that man. He knows how to clean
the street,' and he's likely to walk over and tell him so."
Betty points out the same quality. She remembers taking
singing lessons when she was a child. She wanted to become
a professional singer, but she didn't have the talent. "One
day my father came home early and he heard my voice. He
canceled the lessons immediately. He did not have any
patience for the amateur." As one writer put it, "He has an
inordinate admiration for champions."

He dislikes the overly aggressive and pushy people who
"try to take over and run things." He also resents the snide
sophisticates and the feeling is often mutual. They think
he is corny and laugh at some of his columns like:

> Listen kids: don't quit. Don't ever become hopelessly dis-
> couraged. Stay in there and keep pitching and trying until
> the last out of the game because anything can happen....
> Next time, when things look bleak and gloomy, remember
> the premiums available to those who refuse to quit. The
> payoff is on courage; cowardice never collects at the payoff
> windows....

Sullivan is more interested in content than style and is
contemptuous of people who sneer at sincere sentiment because of the phrasing. He can be sophisticated himself if he
chooses, making wry and witty observations. He talks dryly
about the bags under his eyes: "People say they give me
character. Who the hell wants character?" He gives a perfect
imitation of the enthusiastic, homespun warm-up delivered
by his announcer Ralph Paul before the show. However,
few people are aware of this, least of all Paul, because Sul-

livan doesn't show this side of his personality at the studio
and, besides, during the warm-up he is in the wings where
voices from the stage don't carry.

His closest friends are warm and not slick and few of them
are entertainers. He has met the elite of the country—the
social, political and business leaders—but does not socialize
with them. David Granger is a stock broker in his thirties.
Other friends are his contemporaries and people he has
known well for years. Joan and Benny Gaines own a motel
in Florida, and their friendship dates back to the Loew's
State days when Mrs. Gaines appeared in Sullivan's stage
shows under the name of Joan Abbott. Another close friend,
Jerry Brady, has known Sullivan since boyhood when he
was a basketball and baseball star for Yonkers High School.
The inner circle also includes clothing manufacturer Vin
Draddy, toy manufacturer David Marx, real-estate man
Lewis Lubitz, Morris Uchitel of El Morocco and Sylvia
Sokolow and Mrs. Walter T. Shirley, widows whose hus-
bands were also friends of the Sullivans. Sullivan's first two
good friends when he came to New York were the late boxer
Johnny Dundee, who was a witness at his wedding, and Joe
Moore, one of America's outstanding speed skaters. These
are friendships that lasted more than four decades.

Ed Sullivan's best friend is his audience. He walks down
the street and says Hello to the people he passes in a sincere and open way. If they don't respond, he will probably
say Hello a second time. He finds genuine pleasure from
these contacts and never acts like a celebrity with his fans
but a man meeting friends. He prefers to have strangers call
him Ed and not Mr. Sullivan, and they do. Doormen, labor-
ers, cabdrivers, people looking out of windows, all yell out
cheerful greetings when they see him and he responds: "Hi.

How are you today?" He will walk into a restaurant and nod to the waiter: "Hi there, young fella." His manner is genial but never condescending. He is happy when other people behave that way too and aren't overly attentive or deferential. A bartender will ask how he feels and he will enjoy exchanging the small talk. "Fine, just fine," will be the jovial answer. "Woke up with a little crimp in my neck, though." This is probably the first time in the day that he has confided to anyone that small fact about his health. Oddly he is more apt to reveal personal details to strangers than friends.

He is never too busy to stop and sign autographs, unlike many stars who prefer to be shielded from the public. He has unlimited patience and will stand on the street writing his name longer than any other reasonable man. He will not merely put down his signature but ask for the name or birthdate or hometown and write something personal. Observers were struck in Florida when he was with Frank Sinatra who avoided the crowds while Sullivan stayed behind and kept on writing.

At Expo 67 he taped an aerial act and afterward thousands of fans descended upon him. He started signing autographs, but he was soon encircled and trapped and the police had to free him so he could make his next appointment.

He often receives the most attention in foreign countries, frequently from Americans abroad who are happy to see that familiar face from the United States. On a trip to Germany he dropped in at a West Berlin nightclub to look over the talent. The place was a popular rendezvous for American GI's who flocked to his table as soon as they spotted him. Many of them asked him to relay messages to their families and girl friends in the United States, and he did.

Certain remarks are repeated regularly by strangers who think they are being original. Most common are, "You'd better get back to the show, Smiley," "Hey, Eddie, keesa me good-night," and the observation that television should be called Sullivision. Autograph seekers say: "Do you mind signing this on a check?" His standard answer: "If you can cash it, I get ten percent."

Once he was in the Vatican listening to the guide when a woman whispered, "You'd better get back to the show, Smiley."

His offhand conversations help Sullivan to keep the pulse of the public, and comments from strangers have an enormous impact on the content of the show—more than on any other television program. He is also influenced by people who phone and write letters, especially when a large number are in favor of or against the same thing.

Of course there is always "nut" mail, which is disregarded. "I am firmly convinced that there are people who make a career of sitting in front of TV sets making minute notes on everything they see. If they find fifteen objectionable seconds in an hour's show they sit down and write furious complaining letters about those fifteen seconds."

Most of the letters ask for photographs, which Carmine provides, or tickets, and these are forwarded to the CBS ticket office. Because of the tremendous demand the program is generally booked up six months in advance. Occasionally Carmine will read some letter that hits a soft spot and he will also send tickets. There is a steady stream of mail but it reached avalanche proportions at the time of

Sullivan's automobile accident in 1956 and during the Beatles' appearances.

The customer is always right on "The Ed Sullivan Show."

"Always trust your audience with a show. It sounds corn-ball but it's true. I have a profound respect for an audience. We work like hell week after week and then await the verdict. They will tell you right away if something is not up to par."

He has relied on his studio audience to find out the strengths and weaknesses of a program since he first went on the air. The "out-of-town tryout" is the Sunday after-noon dress rehearsal. The people in the theater become a miniature sample of the audience at home, a sort of pre-air Neilsen rating. "People are people the world over. . . . There are certain universals. . . . Tastes are the same every-where. . . . The audience response in the afternoon is the same as it would be on the actual show and with any audience."

Sullivan admires the George Arliss statement that when people are assembled together "their mass instinct is peril-ously close to intelligence."

He chats with the audience in a pleasant, relaxed way. He is solicitous about their comfort and makes certain the television monitors are placed so everyone can view the taped segments easily. For all his consideration he still po-litely but firmly demands quiet from an unruly crowd. When teen-agers continue to scream, he scolds them like a fond but irritated parent.

While a set is being changed, he carries on a homey, small-town kind of conversation. He asks what part of the country they are from and what performers they like. He advises visitors to the city to see the ships in the harbor and, during Christmas, the trees along Park Avenue and at Rockefeller Center. Sometimes he talks about the television equipment—the boom and teleprompter—and describes what happens in the control room. He enjoys these exchanges. "I always had a nice feeling with audiences. I never went out scared of them."

Often he displays more intimacy with his audience than with his close friends. The public is a companion he likes and trusts and sometimes confides in ahead of his business associates. It is not unusual for the staff to find out about a booking first when they hear him announce it in the theater.

These people in the studio have waited for months to see the Sullivan show. They stand in line outside The Ed Sullivan Theater at 53rd Street and Broadway. There are women from out of town wearing white hats and white shoes and young couples from Queens all dressed up in their Sunday best. There are long-haired teen-agers with transistors and portable phonographs and little children tightly holding their mothers' hands. There are servicemen and elderly people and women wearing hair curlers and bored middle-aged men. There are no tuxedoes or evening clothes or diamonds in this cross section of middle-class America. As newcomers arrive and get into the back of the line, they are approached for tickets by the weekly regulars and the autograph hounds and the fans of that evening's rock-and-roll group, and now and then someone has an extra one to hand out.

From the outside the building looks like any of the dozens of New York legitimate theaters and that is exactly what it was when it opened up on November 30, 1927, as Hammerstein's Theatre with a play called *The Golden Dawn*. Since then the house has had a checkered history. In 1931

it was renamed the Manhattan Theatre, in 1934 the Billy
Rose Music Hall, eight months later the Manhattan Theatre again, until February, 1936, when it became the WPA
Theatre. In July, 1936, CBS took it over and converted it
to a radio theater and with the advent of television re-
christened it Studio 50. In January, 1953, it became the
home of the Sullivan show and on December 10, 1967, it
received its latest name, The Ed Sullivan Theater, to honor
the host's twentieth year.

At 12:15 the ticket holders for the dress rehearsal enter
the theater. These include friends of the sponsors and cast
whose names are at the door and who will be given preferred
locations. Outside there are people without tickets waiting
in the hope there will be empty seats and they will be
admitted at the last moment.

The lobby is large but the orchestra is much smaller than
a conventional-sized theater because renovation first for
television and then for color has drastically reduced the
seating capacity. In 1927 well over a thousand people could
be accommodated, but today there is room for only 570. The
orchestra has been sliced down the middle, and on the left
side are seats. The right is occupied by the control room,
the band and an extension of the stage. Above is a large
balcony, the front of which was once a loge, but now holds
lighting equipment, including the spotlights. Overhead the
high domed ceiling is almost all that remains to betray that
this was built for another age.

After the audience is seated, Ed Sullivan's taped voice
is heard over the loudspeaker. "Good evening, ladies and
gentlemen. We're delighted to have you in our theater tonight. While waiting for the clock to strike eight, you'll be
entertained by recordings of some of the stars...." Of course

the clock is not going to strike eight, but there is only one tape and it is used both in the afternoon and the evening. Sullivan introduces a succession of records including Johnny Ray singing "Cry," Elvis Presley's "Hound Dog," Nancy Sinatra with "These Boots Were Made for Walkin'," Barry Sadler's "The Green Beret," Anthony Newley with his version of "Bye Bye Blackbird," Jimmy Durante and "Old Man Time."

Onstage there is activity. The scenic designer walks briskly toward the control room. Heading in the opposite direction is a secretary with a pencil in her mouth and a notebook in her hand. The lighting director makes last-minute adjustments. Cameramen focus on test patterns and on a blonde girl in a red dress and black stockings. She is the "color girl" and stands onstage quietly while men in the control room check her on their monitors and adjust the color.

All of the current movement has followed a busy week in which the producer and his staff have worked out the program in detail. They have determined the sets, the songs, the costumes, the lighting, the choreography. The dancers have rehearsed for many days, but the other performers have probably had one meeting during the week at the program's office.

By Friday production numbers have been blocked and the show is fairly well set. At 10 A.M. on Saturday the first studio rehearsal, the "first fax," begins, and all the elements of the production except for the orchestra are together for the first time. Camera angles and moves, which previously had been estimated, are now worked out in the studio. Afterward the orchestra rehearses with each of the featured performers. By 6 P.M. the studio is quiet again until Sunday at

9 A.M. when the acts have additional rehearsals before the
1 P.M. dress.

Ed Sullivan starts off Sunday with his usual lamb chop
and then goes to work on the column. Someone else might be
tempted to write it the night before instead of the morning
of the busiest day, but in print as well as on television he
insists on being spontaneous and up-to-the-minute. Carmine
arrives from his Bronx home and dispatches his boss to the
studio and the column to the *News*.

Joe Moore drives Sullivan to the studio in his Lincoln,
license plate 1-M (Sullivan's own Lincoln has license ES).
On the way they pass the main entrance of the theater with
its new name emblazoned out front. The marquee has the
guests on the show that evening, some listed by their full
names, others by abbreviation or last name only. The exact
billing and phrasing has been determined in advance by the
host, one more example of his involvement in every aspect
of the show.

Around 1 P.M. the automobile stops in front of the stage
door at 219 West 53rd Street and the passenger steps out.
He is wearing buckled loafers—his favorite pair was a
present from George Hamilton after Sullivan admired the
shoes on the actor. In his left hand he is carrying a newly
pressed suit on a wire hanger which he will put on immediately before air time. Like all of his suits, it is from
Dunhill Tailors and has an identifying number on the
inside, as do all his ties. The production staff keeps a record
of the suit and tie number for each show, so when he reuses
an old tape or delivers new introductions for his rebroadcast
programs, it is easy to match up outfits and avoid different
clothes on one show.

Sullivan pauses on the sidewalk, still holding the suit, and signs autographs for the teen-agers who have stopped him. Then he opens the door to 219 and enters a small enclosure with another door and a glass partition on the right, which enables the guard inside to check on new arrivals. Sullivan walks through the second door and, ignoring the elevator straight ahead, climbs up the stairs in front and a little to the left. "Hi there," he says to the guard. He does not let anyone take the suit but carries it up the stairs himself, one flight to 21, his dressing room.

The large outer room has a sofa, chairs, tables, typewriters and a television set. This is where the secretaries work and where some of the production staff gather before the show. At the far end of the room is another door which leads to a small cubicle, just big enough for a desk, chair and bed. This is the star's dressing room, but the only sign of status is a private bathroom. Sullivan has had nothing to do with the layout and decor, but the lack of ostentation suits his style. The room is as unpretentious as the man.

There is a quick makeup job and a last-minute conference and then he heads down the stairs and waits backstage for his cue. Out front the audience cannot tell that he has just arrived, but there is a slight quickening of the pre-rehearsal pace. The cameramen are suddenly all in place and set to go. There is no more brisk or casual walking across the stage. Soon the tape of Sullivan's voice and the records stop. There is a mood of readiness.

Sullivan stands backstage waiting to go on. He is by himself, hunched over, concentrating, buried in thought, remote, unapproachable. He displays none of the casualness that was evident earlier while he was signing autographs. He has retreated inside himself to reflect on some aspect of the show he will soon judge with dispassionate objectivity and dissect with a surgeon's precision.

Around him stagehands are moving equipment into place, a female singer is checking her eye makeup in a mirror, an electrician is pulling switches, a comedian is going over his lines and jumps aside as the set for the opening number descends near him. Sullivan seems unaware of the activity but he knows what is going on. This is part of his "estate" and he is familiar with every aspect of the terrain. He no longer needs to survey the property to know that it extends farther than the eye can see.

This will be the first time he has looked at the performers in their completed routines, giving him "the advantage of a fresh, objective view along with the benefit of the reaction in the studio." Some of the acts he has never seen at all, and some performers nobody on the show has seen until the first meeting a few days before air. One was the New Vaudeville Band, an English group booked because of their successful record "Winchester Cathedral." Their photographs weren't even available, and it was a pleasant surprise when they turned out to be attractive youngsters and not old men, the least embarrassing possibility that was jokingly considered.

Onstage, announcer Ralph Paul is warming up the audience. He points toward the color girl at his left and says, "If you have a color set at home and you get a perfect picture it's partly because of our color girl. . . . I'm here to ask for applause. Sometimes people forget to applaud. I'm here to ask that you don't. That's the sound a performer needs. Let's try it now. I'd like you to sound like fifty million people in Madison Square Garden. When I say 'here he is, live from New York, Ed Sullivan,' let's have the ap-

plause. . . . Say Hello to the person on your left and to the
person on your right. Shake hands and get acquainted." He
now introduces Bob Precht, director Tim Kiley and Ray
Bloch. The stage manager emerges from the wings wearing
earphones and Ralph Paul retreats to his corner all the way
on the left where he puts on his own earphones and prepares
to announce the opening. The rehearsal has started and will
proceed exactly as if it were the regular show.

"Tonight from The Ed Sullivan Theater on Broadway,
'The Ed Sullivan Show,'. . . And now, live from New York,
Ed Sullivan." As the announcer says "live," on screen there
is a tape of Sullivan walking on stage. His entrance on
television is never "live." At the same time the host emerges
from the wings in person to the loud applause of the
audience, and the camera picks him up after he is positioned
on the left of the stage. He delivers his opening talk which
usually includes highlights of the week. He has written it
himself and it is in front of him on the teleprompter, but
that won't prevent his ad-libbing and making a mistake.

There is a special electricity when he is onstage which
people only find apparent when he is sick and another performer substitutes as host. Then it is obvious that his enthusiasm is contagious and he makes the acts seem more
exciting.

During the rehearsal he stands on the side, watching the
entertainers. Sometimes he will ask a question of the assistant producer next to him or speak to the teleprompter man
or walk to the wings, but most of the time he stays in place
and gives the acts his complete concentration. It is a courtesy
he feels every performer deserves. He is particularly attentive to comedians because he doesn't want any movement of
his to distract the audience or the comics and ruin a routine.

At these times he gets especially irritated when stagehands make noise or a still photographer darts about in the audience.

He is aware that everyone pays particular notice to his expressions to see if he approves, but he is not self-conscious and does not reveal very much. It is hard to tell from his face if he dislikes an act, but unless something is off-color he is certain to appreciate what the audience enjoys. At rehearsal he carefully measures the mood in the theater and has a double reaction to a comedy line, first an amused chuckle and then a heartier laugh as the audience responds. Many of the talent agents consider themselves expert Sullivan watchers and capable of discerning his opinion. He is supposed to reveal his distaste by drawing back the corners of his mouth very slightly. More than one agent has said that "a certain pursing of the lips is the kiss of death."

Frequently he will call over an entertainer and talk to him, usually because he enjoyed the act but sometimes because there is extra time. Performers like this personal touch because it gives them status. An afternoon ad lib with someone may become part of the evening script, but there is no guarantee he will bring over a person at night, when it counts, just because he did so earlier.

After the rehearsal Sullivan revamps the show. "Bob will have determined possible cuts in the performers' routines and Ray will have outlined musical cuts in anticipation of the problems of time."

It is not just a matter of too long a show. "I rearrange the acts in a different order to develop the pace ... with a newspaper makeup man's feel." The lineup is determined not only by his instincts as a showman but by practical considerations as well. The stage crew needs enough time to set up for a big production number and to clear away the props and scenery afterward. Technical reasons may prevent him from putting on a dance act late in the show.

Usually he meets personally with the top-name comedians whose routines did not work and tells them how much to cut and where to cut it. He has an ingenious knack for saving a disastrous act, and a nine-minute comedy spot that didn't get laughs may work beautifully in four when Sullivan's blue pencil is through with it. He will do anything he feels is necessary to make the show a good one. Says Jack Carter, "Sure he's tough to work for. He's tough as hell. He has a right to be. It's his show and obviously his way works."

His way will even include changing the costumes. On one occasion the McGuire Sisters wore outfits at dress rehearsal that did not photograph well on camera and he wanted something different for the nighttime show. All of the singers' clothes, designed by Sophie of Saks, were locked up in the vault at Saks Fifth Avenue, which was closed on Sunday. Sullivan phoned the manager and asked him to open up the store at six o'clock so the McGuire Sisters could get new wardrobes for the show.

Up in his dressing room Sullivan will make his revisions. "Cut the magician down to three minutes. The start of his act was lousy." The singer will get an extra song. The dance number is cut and moved from the opening spot to the very end. There are no consistent programming rules, but the act he likes least generally closes the show. It's too late for channel switching, and if the program runs long, the number is expendable.

He will dictate new introductions for himself: "All right, now read that back to me...right there now, just add 'We have some stunning girls on the show tonight!'...Get that word stunning in there. . . . What song is he going to sing first? Oh, yeah, that's his big hit, huh?"

Later he may have additional thoughts on the introductions and the running orders, and as the day progresses the secretaries will type up revision number two, three, four, etc.

An hour after the dress he finishes going over the show. It's around four o'clock and he leaves for lunch with Joe Moore, who makes a point of not talking to him about the program. "Eddie wants to relax. He likes to get his mind off the show and think about other things." After the meal Sullivan goes for a brisk walk, comes back to the studio around six and may make additional changes. Then he takes a nap.

Afterward the visitors to his dressing room include his makeup man and people who are to be introduced from the audience, who do not come to the dress rehearsal. He is usually relaxed at this time, unless there are "superstars" on the show and he is especially concerned about everything going right. He spent a long while pacing back and forth in his dressing room before the show when Bob Hope and Bing Crosby were his guests.

Downstairs strangers are likely to show up at the stage door with notes Sullivan has written for them at lunch requesting they be admitted to the program. After the proper scrutiny to make certain that the handwriting is authentic, the visitors will be directed around to the front of the theater and given special treatment. By quarter of eight everyone is in place including the celebrities in the audience whose seats were taped off earlier so the director and cameramen will know where to point the cameras.

Sullivan comes downstairs a few minutes before eight but does not see the audience until he is introduced. There is now a certain tension in the air, an electricity that goes with a live performance.

Sullivan says, "I prefer a live show because you get a sense of immediacy. Late developments—in sports or in the entertainment world—are all grist for the mill. And people make mistakes. On taped and filmed shows the mistakes are carefully edited and the shows come out looking very slick. They don't look natural."

Backstage the telephone bell is turned off. The screen is dark on the television monitors positioned around the theater: three overhead RCA color TV sets downstairs, others spread around the studio, and in the balcony an enormous screen, "the largest in the world," according to Ralph Paul.

In the main control room, the producer, the director, the associate producer, the assistant director, the technical director, the program coordinator are all seated. The "A.D." will set up the shots for the director who will cue the "T.D." to punch them up. The room is filled with monitors in color and black and white. In front are five screens with pictures from the five cameras and a sixth with the on-the-air picture. At thirty seconds to air the room quiets down. The talk now is technical. "Ready your light cue. Artie, open your mike. Open your hard wall. Fly in the cellophane. Music. Hit it."

"... And now, live from New York..." In forty million homes there is one picture of Ed Sullivan. In the studio, there are hundreds. Television screen: tape of Sullivan making his entrance. Onstage: Sullivan actually walking out. Camera one: close-up of Sullivan's face. Camera two: long shot. Camera three: looking up through the audience.

Sullivan speaks, his face serious and intense, and dozens

of Ed Sullivans talk to the audience on monitors around the studio. He is the center of attention. He moves his hand and the effect is dramatic on screen. But in the theater, the gesture is barely noticeable. There he is not even the most prominent figure on stage. He is standing off on the side, marginal and secondary to a comedian seated in the middle of the stage in an imposing set waiting for his cue.

Sullivan finishes the introduction, the cameras shift and the comic begins his routine. During the actual program it becomes evident that Ed Sullivan thoroughly enjoys watching "The Ed Sullivan Show." He literally bends with the acrobats and he responds to the jokes of the comics. Most of the time, the audience at home does not see him roar with laughter. Occasionally the director shows reaction shots. Inside the control room Sullivan is smiling in profile, straight on, and in a long shot with the comedian. "Ready camera one head to toe. Take one. Ready camera four chest shot. A little more profile. Take four. Ready camera two. Take two. Ready one. Take one." Sullivan's laughter is a small part of the action onstage, but it dominates the set with infectious good humor. Monitors around the studio and inside the control room are covered by an enormous grin. In the balcony on the largest screen in the world is a ten-foot smile of Ed Sullivan, larger than any human being, and it overpowers and overwhelms the tiny people in the theater.

When the program is over, Sullivan poses for still photographs with performers, friends in the studio and people he has introduced from the audience. Then he makes two phone calls from backstage, one to Joe Moore and one to his wife. He asks how the show went, but he doesn't really want to know. What he is looking for is reassurance. "Sylvia never makes any criticism Sunday evening. She knows that the last thing you want to hear when you walk off that stage Sunday night was that the show was bad. But a few days later, around Tuesday, she may make a comment about a costume being bad or the lighting being off, but she's always the diplomat."

Mrs. Sullivan hardly ever comes to the theater but watches on her color television set at home with Betty. "I want to see the show the way it comes over the screen," she says. She prefers not having any outsiders present to distract her. In fact, she and Betty talk very little between eight and nine, because they are concentrating on the program. After two decades she still does not relax completely on Sunday night. "It seems that every program is like an opening night. I still get nervous before the show."

The audience pours out of the theater onto Broadway. Stagehands dismantle the scenery, musicians snap shut trumpet and trombone cases, and for one more week the glamor is packed away.

Sullivan heads upstairs again to his dressing room and comes down a moment later—no trailing entourage to proclaim his status. In his left hand is the suit he wore to the studio in the afternoon. The hanger is the same plain wire one. The solitary figure carrying his own suit walks out the stage door by himself.

A group of teen-agers are waiting and they stop him. A girl with long brown hair says, "May I have your autograph, Mr. Sullivan?"

"Certainly." He looks around for a pencil and paper and one of the other youngsters hands them to him. "What's your name?" he says to the girl.

"Patricia."

"Patricia what?"

"Patricia Walter."

He writes down on the paper: "To Patricia Walter. My very best wishes to a girl who will grow up to be a very pretty young lady. Ed Sullivan." He hands her back the paper and she blushes. A boy hands him a sheet without saying a word. "What's your name?" Sullivan asks.

"Buddy."

"And when were you born, Buddy?"

"September."

"Is that so? My birthday is in September too." He writes down: "To Buddy, whose birthday is also in September. Ed Sullivan."

"I really liked the show tonight, Ed," says a middle-aged woman who is standing nearby.

"Is that so? What did you like best?"

"The comic. He was real funny."

"And what about you?" Sullivan asks the man standing next to her.

There are people waiting for him. Bob Precht is waiting. The cabdriver is waiting. The Sullivans are going to Danny's Hideaway as usual after the show and Sylvia is waiting for him to pick her up at the apartment. He is busy now, but he will be along as soon as he has finished signing autographs and chatting. This man who lives in a hotel and eats in restaurants enjoyed spending the evening in the living rooms of forty million people. He is still with his viewers, but now he can see their faces. He loses track of the time, and he isn't aware how late he's going to be getting crosstown to the Delmonico. Ed Sullivan is already home.

Picture Credits

Special thanks to Izzy Seigal and Marty Silverstein, manager and production manager of the CBS Photo Department; former CBS-TV picture editor Barrie Richardson; and Milton Glaser and Vincent Ceci of Push Pin Studios.

2¢ per day fine for overdue book
DATE DUE

FEB 3 '70			
GAYLORD			PRINTED IN U.S.A.